Lightweight Django

Julia Elman and Mark Lavin

Beijing · Cambridge · Farnham · Köln · Sebastopol · Tokyo

Lightweight Django

by Julia Elman and Mark Lavin

Copyright © 2015 Julia Elman and Mark Lavin. All rights reserved.

Printed in the United States of America.

Published by O'Reilly Media, Inc., 1005 Gravenstein Highway North, Sebastopol, CA 95472.

O'Reilly books may be purchased for educational, business, or sales promotional use. Online editions are also available for most titles (*http://safaribooksonline.com*). For more information, contact our corporate/institutional sales department: 800-998-9938 or *corporate@oreilly.com*.

Editor: Meghan Blanchette	**Indexer:** Wendy Catalano
Production Editor: Colleen Lobner	**Cover Designer:** Ellie Volckhausen
Copyeditor: Rachel Monaghan	**Interior Designer:** David Futato
Proofreader: Sonia Saruba	**Illustrator:** Rebecca Demarest

November 2014:   First Edition

Revision History for the First Edition:

2014-10-24:   First release

See *http://oreilly.com/catalog/errata.csp?isbn=9781491945940* for release details.

ISBN: 978-1-491-94594-0

LSI

Table of Contents

Preface

Since the creation of Django, a plethora of web frameworks have been created in various open source communities. Frontend-focused web frameworks such as Angular.js, Ember.js, and Backbone.js have come out of the JavaScript community and become forerunners in modern web development. Where does Django fit into all of this? How can we integrate these client-side MVC frameworks into our current Django infrastructure?

Lightweight Django teaches you how to take advantage of Django's Pythonic "batteries included" philosophy. Its aim is to guide you through misconceptions that Django is too "heavy" for rapid application development. From creating the world's smallest Django application to building a RESTful API, *Lightweight Django* will walk you through how to take advantage of this popular Python web framework.

Why This Book?

We wanted to write this book primarily because we love Django. The community is amazing, and there are so many resources to learn about Django and to develop applications using it. However, we also felt like many of these resources, including the official Django documentation, put too much emphasis on the power of Django and not on its decoupled design. Django is a well-written framework, with numerous utilities for building web applications included. What we want this book to highlight is how you can break apart and potentially replace these components to pick and choose what best suits the application you want to build. Similarly, we wanted to break down the typical structure of Django projects and applications. Our goal is to get you to stop asking "how do I do X in Django?" and instead ask "does Django provide anything to help me do X, and if not, is something available in the community?"

In addition, we wanted to answer questions about where Django fits in a Web in which more applications are built with heavy client-side interactions and real-time components, and paired with native mobile applications. As a framework, Django is agnostic about the client, which leaves some users feeling like Django doesn't have an answer for building these types of applications. We hope that this book can help shape how the community approaches these types of problems. We want to see Django and its community continue to grow, and we want to be a part of it for many more years to come.

Who Should Read This Book?

If you are interested in reading this book, you are most likely an intermediate Django user. You've gone through the Django polls tutorial, as well as written a few basic Django web applications, and are now wondering what the next steps are. *Lightweight Django* serves as that next step to help outline how to utilize Django's utilities and simplicity.

Or you might be currently working on a Django project and wondering how to integrate something like Backbone.js into your project. *Lightweight Django* will teach you some best practices for integration and will give you a jumping-off point for building content-rich web applications.

Who Should Not Read This Book?

While we feel that *Lightweight Django* is beneficial to developers from many backgrounds, there might be certain people who won't find this book interesting. For those of you who do not find writing Python and/or JavaScript pleasurable, this book is most likely not for you. All of the concepts and examples revolve around these languages, and they will be heavily used throughout each chapter. We also don't recommend this book for those who are brand new to Django.

About the Examples

Each of the example projects has been carefully crafted under the theme of rapid application development. In each chapter, you'll learn how to build projects that assist with project management, tools, and team collaboration. We wanted our readers to build projects that they find useful and can customize for their own use. In general, if example code is offered with this book, you may use it in your programs and documentation. You do not need to contact us for permission unless you're reproducing a significant portion of the code. For example, writing a program that uses several chunks of code from this book does not require permission. Selling or distributing a CD-ROM of examples from O'Reilly books does require permission. Answering a question by citing this book and quoting example code does not require permission. Incorporating a significant amount of example code from this book into your product's documentation does require permission.

The code samples for this title can be found here: *https://github.com/lightweightdjango/ examples.*

We appreciate, but do not require, attribution. An attribution usually includes the title, author, publisher, and ISBN. For example: "*Lightweight Django* by Julia Elman and Mark Lavin (O'Reilly). Copyright 2015 Julia Elman and Mark Lavin, 978-1-491-94594-0."

If you feel your use of code examples falls outside fair use or the permission given above, feel free to contact us at *permissions@oreilly.com*.

Organization of This Book

Chapter 1, The World's Smallest Django Project

Creating lightweight and simple web applications is the core concept in this book. In this chapter, you'll be building a runnable, single-file "Hello World" Django application.

Chapter 2, Stateless Web Application

Ever wonder how placeholder image services are created? Chapter 2 walks you through how to build a stateless web application to generate placeholder image URLs.

Chapter 3, Building a Static Site Generator

Rapid prototyping is a useful technique for creating and scaffolding web applications. We'll review the purposes of this technique by creating a static site generator to help scaffold your team's project.

Chapter 4, Building a REST API

REST APIs are an important part of creating web applications with rich and relevant content. This is the chapter in which we start building out a large-scale Scrum board application by using the `django-rest-framework`.

Chapter 5, Client-Side Django with Backbone.js

Chapter 5 continues with what we built in Chapter 4 by walking you through creating a Backbone.js application that works with our newly made RESTful API. We'll touch on each component that creates a new Backbone application and how to sync up this client-side framework with Django.

Chapter 6, Single-Page Web Application

Single-page web applications are a way in which we can create enriching client-side web applications. In this chapter we'll return to our simple Backbone application and continue our progress by making it a robust single-page application.

Chapter 7, Real-Time Django

Creating web applications that respond to interactions in real time provides instant gratification for our users. To complete our project from the previous two chapters, we'll add a real-time component to our Scrum board using websockets and Tornado, an asynchronous networking library written in Python.

Chapter 8, Communication Between Django and Tornado

Connecting the power of Django to the robust behaviors of Tornado is an important measure in creating scalable, real-time Django applications. In this chapter, we'll expand on our usage of the Tornado server by integrating the ability to work with Django to create a secure and interactive relationship.

Conventions Used in This Book

The following typographical conventions are used in this book:

Italic

Indicates new terms, URLs, email addresses, filenames, and file extensions.

`Constant width`

Used for program listings, as well as within paragraphs to refer to program elements such as variable or function names, databases, data types, environment variables, statements, and keywords.

`Constant width bold`

Shows commands or other text that should be typed literally by the user.

`Constant width italic`

Shows text that should be replaced with user-supplied values or by values determined by context.

Throughout the code examples, we will use an ellipsis (…) to denote that some of the previously displayed content has been skipped to shorten long code examples or to skip to the most relevant section of the code.

 This element signifies a tip or suggestion.

 This element signifies a general note.

 This element indicates a warning or caution.

How to Contact Us

Please address comments and questions concerning this book to the publisher:

O'Reilly Media, Inc.
1005 Gravenstein Highway North
Sebastopol, CA 95472
800-998-9938 (in the United States or Canada)
707-829-0515 (international or local)
707-829-0104 (fax)

We have a web page for this book, where we list errata, examples, and any additional information. You can access this page at *http://www.oreilly.com/catalog/0636920032502.*

To comment or ask technical questions about this book, send email to *lightweightdjango@gmail.com.*

For more information about our books, courses, conferences, and news, see our website at *http://www.oreilly.com.*

Find us on Facebook: *http://facebook.com/oreilly*

Follow us on Twitter: *http://twitter.com/oreillymedia*

Watch us on YouTube: *http://www.youtube.com/oreillymedia*

Acknowledgments

There are numerous people to thank and without whom this book would not be possible. We received amazing support from our editor, Meghan Blanchette.

Thank you to our technical reviewers—Aymeric Augustin, Jon Banafato, Barbara Shaurette, and Marie Selvanadin— for your comments, both positive and negative, which helped to shape and focus the book. Also thank you to Heather Scherer for shepherding the technical review.

We are grateful to all the open source developers and contributors whose endless hours of work were needed to make these tools available for us to use and write about.

Thank you to our early release readers for taking a chance on our unfinished work, dealing with typos and poor formatting, and giving feedback and correcting mistakes.

Julia

I would like to thank my wonderful family and close friends for their support throughout the course of writing this book. To my husband, Andrew, for believing in my abilities, and for his constant encouragement and steadfast support during this long and bumpy journey. To my daughter, Hannah, who is my inspiration and from whom I can always grow my strength every step of the way. To my mother, Katherine, for pushing me beyond what I ever thought I was capable of doing. To my stepfather, Tom, for teaching me how to use a cordless drill, changing the oil in my car, and instilling in me the value of hard work. Thank you to my brother, Alex, and sister, Elizabeth, for always cheering me on from the sidelines. Thank you to my best friend, Jenny, for her constant love and lifelong friendship.

Also, thank you to my wonderful coauthor, Mark, for his brilliance and friendship; he is one of the most talented developers I have ever collaborated with. We made it to this finish line together, and I cannot imagine going through this book writing journey with anyone else.

I'd also like to thank the Python community and a few specific members who have inspired, encouraged, and/or mentored me throughout my career: James Bennett, Sean Bleier, Nathan Borror, Colin Copeland, Matt Croydon, Katie Cunningham, Selena Deckelmann, Jacob Kaplan-Moss, Jessica McKellar, Jesse Noller, Christian Metts, Lynn Root, Caleb Smith, Paul Smith, Karen Tracey, Malcolm Tredinnick, Ben Turner, and Simon Willison.

Mark

First and foremost, this book would not be possible without the love and support of my family. My wife, Beth, and daughter, Kennedy, put up with long hours and a grumpier and more stressed version of me than they deserve. Also thanks to my brother, Matt, for his insight and early feedback. Thank you to my parents and my brother James for their lifetime of support.

Thank you to my coauthor, Julia. Our collaboration is a celebration of our friendship and mutual respect. I will forever cherish our ability to work together to create something greater than the sum of our contributions.

Finally, thank you to my coworkers at Caktus Group for your support in time, feedback, and encouragement.

Prerequisites

Before we dive in, this chapter is an outline of the knowledge and software requirements you'll need to follow the examples in this book.

Python

This book is aimed at developers with at least some previous Python experience, and in this book we are using Python 3. In particular, the examples have been tested to run on Python 3.3 and 3.4. Those familiar enough with Python may be able to work through this book using Python 2.7, converting the example code as needed, though it is not recommended. To read more about what is new in these versions of Python and to find installation instructions for your system, visit *https://www.python.org/downloads/*.

We expect that you have Python installed on your local development machine, know how to edit Python files, and know how to run them. Throughout this book, when we reference Python on the command line, we will use `python`, though some systems or installations may require using `python3` or the full version, such as `python3.3` or `python3.4`. Similarly, when installing new packages, the examples will use `pip` (*https://pypi.python.org/pypi/pip*), though some installations may require using `pip3`. For this book, and Python development in general, it is recommended that you create an isolated Python environment for each project using `virtualenv` (*https://pypi.python.org/pypi/virtualenv*). Without an isolated environment, installing new Python packages with `pip` may require root access or administrative rights on your computer. We'll assume that if this is the case, you will prefix the `pip` command with `sudo` or any other commands you may need to gain such rights, but those prefixes will not be shown in the examples.

Python Packages

The only Python package that is required before you start this book is Django. All of the examples have been tested and written to work with Django 1.7. It is recommended that you install with pip:

```
hostname $ pip install Django==1.7
```

 As of August 2014, Django 1.7 was still in a release candidate phase. If the preceding installation does not work, you can install the 1.7 pre-release from the development branch with pip install https://github.com/django/django/archive/stable/1.7.x.zip.

To read more about what is new in this version of Django, visit *https://docs.djangoproject.com/en/dev/releases/1.7/*. For additional installation instructions, you can also see the Django guide on installation (*https://docs.djangoproject.com/en/1.7/intro/install/*).

Additional packages will be installed throughout the chapters. Chapters 1, 2, and 3 are each independent projects and can be treated as separate virtual environments, again with Django being the only prerequisite. Chapters 4 through 8 comprise one large project, and the same virtual environment should be used for those chapters.

Web Development

As Django is a web framework, this book assumes you have some basic knowledge of HTML and CSS. The JavaScript examples are more in depth, and the expected level of knowledge is detailed more in the following section. A basic understanding of the HTTP protocol, in particular the usage and purpose of the various HTTP verbs (GET, POST, PUT, DELETE, etc.), is helpful.

JavaScript

The later chapters in this book make heavy use of JavaScript. You should also be familiar with writing JavaScript/jQuery. A developer experienced doing DOM manipulation and making AJAX calls with jQuery should be able to follow the examples using Backbone.js. If you are familiar with another client-side framework such as Angular.js, Ember.js, or Knockout.js, you will be ahead of the game. This is not meant to be a definitive guide on Backbone.js. If you are not familiar with working with JavaScript, and Backbone.js MVC architecture in particular, here are some recommended O'Reilly titles for you to read:

- JavaScript: The Definitive Guide (*http://shop.oreilly.com/product/9780596805531.do*), by David Flanagan (2011)
- JavaScript: The Good Parts (*http://shop.oreilly.com/product/9780596517748.do*), by Douglas Crockford (2008)
- JavaScript Patterns (*http://shop.oreilly.com/product/9783897215986.do*), by Stoyan Stefanov (2010)
- Speaking JavaScript (*http://shop.oreilly.com/product/0636920029564.do*), by Axel Rauschmayer (2014)
- Developing Backbone.js Applications (*http://shop.oreilly.com/product/0636920025344.do*), by Addy Osmani (2013)

Browser Support

The examples in this book make use of relatively new HTML5 and CSS3 APIs, and expect a modern browser. Anything below these versions has not been tested thoroughly and/or may not support the technology that we use in the examples:

- IE 10+
- Firefox 28.0+
- Chrome 33.0+

You should be familiar with using the developer tools in your preferred browser to debug potential errors, see network requests, and use the JavaScript console.

Additional Software

Later chapters will make use of two popular databases: PostgreSQL and Redis. Brief installation instructions are noted in the chapters where needed, but you should refer to the official documentation for a more complete guide for your system.

PostgreSQL (*http://www.postgresql.org/*) is an open source relational database system that has strong support in the Django community. Any version of PostgreSQL supported by Django will work for this book. Django 1.7 supports PostgreSQL 8.4 and higher.

Redis (*http://redis.io/*) is an open source key/value cache. This book makes use of the pub/sub features of Redis and requires 2.0 and higher.

CHAPTER 1

The World's Smallest Django Project

How many of our journeys into using Django have begun with the official polls tutorial? For many it seems like a rite of passage, but as an introduction to Django it is a fairly daunting task. With various commands to run and files to generate, it is even harder to tell the difference between a project and an application. For new users wanting to start building applications with Django, it begins to feel far too "heavy" as an option for a web framework. What are some ways we can ease these new users' fears to create a clean and simple start?

Let's take a moment to consider the recommended tasks for starting a Django project. The creation of a new project generally starts with the `startproject` command. There is no real magic to what this command does; it simply creates a few files and directories.

While the `startproject` command is a useful tool, it is not required in order to start a Django project. You are free to lay out your project however you like based on what you want to do. For larger projects, developers benefit from the code organization provided by the `startproject` command. However, the convenience of this command shouldn't stop you from understanding what it does and why it is helpful.

In this chapter we'll lay out an example of how to create a simple project using Django's basic building blocks. This lightweight "Hello World" project will create a simple Django application using a single-file approach.

Hello Django

Building a "Hello World" example in a new language or framework is a common first project. We've seen this simple starter project example come out of the Flask community to display how lightweight it is as a microframework.

In this chapter, we'll start by using a single *hello.py* file. This file will contain all of the code needed to run our Django project. In order to have a full working project, we'll need to create a view to serve the root URL and the necessary settings to configure the Django environment.

Creating the View

Django is referred to as a *model-template-view* (MTV) framework. The view portion typically inspects the incoming HTTP request and queries, or constructs, the necessary data to send to the presentation layer.

In our example *hello.py* file, let's create a simple way to execute a "Hello World" response.

```
from django.http import HttpResponse


def index(request):
    return HttpResponse('Hello World')
```

In a larger project, this would typically be in a *views.py* file inside one of your apps. However, there is no requirement for views to live inside of apps. There is also no requirement that views live in a file called *views.py*. This is purely a matter of convention, but not a requirement on which to base our project's structure.

The URL Patterns

In order to tie our view into the site's structure, we'll need to associate it with a URL pattern. For this example, the server root can serve the view on its own. Django associates views with their URL by pairing a regular expression to match the URL and any callable arguments to the view. The following is an example from *hello.py* of how we make this connection.

```
from django.conf.urls import url
from django.http import HttpResponse


def index(request):
    return HttpResponse('Hello World')


urlpatterns = (
    url(r'^$', index),
)
```

Now this file combines both a typical *views.py* file and the root *urls.py* file. Again, it is worth noting that there is no requirement for the URL patterns to be included in a *urls.py* file. They can live in any importable Python module.

Let's move on to our Django settings and the simple lines we'll need to make our project runnable.

The Settings

Django settings detail everything from database and cache connections to internationalization features and static and uploaded resources. For many developers just getting started, the settings in Django are a major point of confusion. While recent releases have worked to trim down the default settings' file length, it can still be overwhelming.

This example will run Django in debugging mode. Beyond that, Django merely needs to be configured to know where the root URLs can be found and will use the value defined by the urlpatterns variable in that module. In this example from *hello.py*, the root URLs are in the current module and will use the urlpatterns defined in the previous section.

```
from django.conf import settings


settings.configure(
    DEBUG=True,
    SECRET_KEY='thisisthesecretkey',
    ROOT_URLCONF=__name__,
    MIDDLEWARE_CLASSES=(
        'django.middleware.common.CommonMiddleware',
        'django.middleware.csrf.CsrfViewMiddleware',
        'django.middleware.clickjacking.XFrameOptionsMiddleware',
    ),
)
...
```

 This example includes a nonrandom SECRET_KEY setting, which should not be used in a production environment. A secret key must be generated for the default session and cross-site request forgery (CSRF) protection. It is important for any production site to have a random SECRET_KEY that is kept private. To learn more, go to the documentation at *https://docs.djangoproject.com/en/1.7/topics/signing/*.

We need to configure the settings before making any additional imports from Django, as some parts of the framework expect the settings to be configured before they are imported. Normally, this wouldn't be an issue since these settings would be included in their own *settings.py* file. The file generated by the default startproject command would also include settings for things that aren't used by this example, such as the internationalization and static resources.

Running the Example

Let's take a look at what our example looks like during `runserver`. A typical Django project contains a *manage.py* file, which is used to run various commands such as creating database tables and running the development server. This file itself is a total of 10 lines of code. We'll be adding in the relevant portions of this file into our *hello.py* to create the same abilities *manage.py* has:

```python
import sys


from django.conf import settings


settings.configure(
    DEBUG=True,
    SECRET_KEY='thisisthesecretkey',
    ROOT_URLCONF=__name__,
    MIDDLEWARE_CLASSES=(
        'django.middleware.common.CommonMiddleware',
        'django.middleware.csrf.CsrfViewMiddleware',
        'django.middleware.clickjacking.XFrameOptionsMiddleware',
    ),
)


from django.conf.urls import url
from django.http import HttpResponse


def index(request):
    return HttpResponse('Hello World')


urlpatterns = (
    url(r'^$', index),
)


if __name__ == "__main__":
    from django.core.management import execute_from_command_line

    execute_from_command_line(sys.argv)
```

Now you can start the example in the command line:

```
hostname $ python hello.py runserver
Performing system checks...

System check identified no issues (0 silenced).
August 06, 2014 - 19:15:36
Django version 1.7c2, using settings None
```

```
Starting development server at http://7.0.0.1:8000/
Quit the server with CONTROL-C.
```

and visit *http://localhost:8000/* in your favorite browser to see "Hello World," as seen in Figure 1-1.

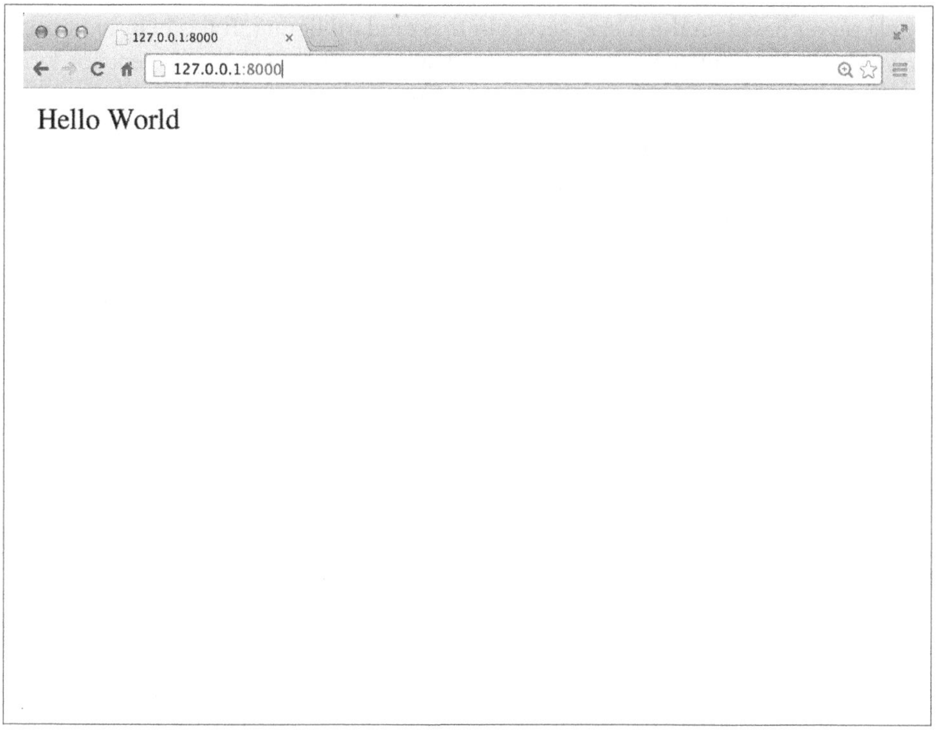

Figure 1-1. Hello World

Now that we have a very basic file structure in place, let's move on to adding more elements to serve up our files.

Improvements

This example shows some of the fundamental pieces of the Django framework: writing views, creating settings, and running management commands. At its core, Django is a Python framework for taking incoming HTTP requests and returning HTTP responses. What happens in between is up to you.

Django also provides additional utilities for common tasks involved in handling HTTP requests, such as rendering HTML, parsing form data, and persisting session state. While not required, it is important to understand how these features can be used in your application in a lightweight manner. By doing so, you gain a better understanding of the overall Django framework and true capabilities.

WSGI Application

Currently, our "Hello World" project runs through the `runserver` command. This is a simple server based on the socket server in the standard library. It has helpful utilities for local development such as auto–code reloading. While it is convenient for local development, `runserver` is not appropriate for production deployment security.

The Web Server Gateway Interface (WSGI) is the specification for how web servers communicate with application frameworks such as Django, and was defined by PEP 333 and improved in PEP 3333. There are numerous choices for web servers that speak WSGI, including Apache via mod_wsgi, Gunicorn, uWSGI, CherryPy, Tornado, and Chaussette.

Each of these servers needs a properly defined WSGI application to be used. Django has an easy interface for creating this application through `get_wsgi_application`.

```
...
from django.conf.urls import url
from django.core.wsgi import get_wsgi_application
from django.http import HttpResponse
...
application = get_wsgi_application()

if __name__ == "__main__":
    from django.core.management import execute_from_command_line

    execute_from_command_line(sys.argv)
```

This would normally be contained within the *wsgi.py* file created by the `startproject` command. The name *application* is merely a convention used by most WSGI servers; each provides configuration options to use a different name if needed.

Now our simple Django project is ready for the WSGI server. Gunicorn is a popular choice for a pure-Python WSGI application server; it has a solid performance record, is easy to install, and also runs on Python 3. Gunicorn can be installed via the Python Package Index (`pip`).

```
hostname $ pip install gunicorn
```

Once Gunicorn is installed, you can run it fairly simply by using the `gunicorn` command.

```
hostname $ gunicorn hello --log-file=-
[2014-08-06 19:17:26 -0400] [37043] [INFO] Starting gunicorn 19.1.1
[2014-08-06 19:17:26 -0400] [37043] [INFO]
    Listening at: http://127.0.0.1:8000 (37043)
```

```
[2014-08-06 19:17:26 -0400] [37043] [INFO] Using worker: sync
[2014-08-06 19:17:26 -0400] [37046] [INFO] Booting worker with pid: 37046
```

As seen in the output, this example is running using Gunicorn version 19.1.1. The timestamps shown contain your time zone offset, which may differ depending on your locale. The process IDs for the arbiter and the worker will also be different.

As of R19, Gunicorn no longer logs to the console by default. Adding the `--log-file=-` option ensures that the output will be logged to the console. You can read more about Gunicorn settings at *http://docs.gunicorn.org/en/19.1/*.

As with `runserver` in Django, the server is listening on *http://127.0.0.1:8000/*. This works out nicely and makes an easier configuration for us to work with.

Additional Configuration

While Gunicorn is a production-ready web server, the application itself is not yet production ready, as DEBUG should never be enabled in production. As previously noted, the SECRET_KEY is also nonrandom and should be made random for additional security.

For more information on the security implications of the DEBUG and SECRET_KEY settings, please refer to the official Django documentation (*https://docs.djangoproject.com/en/1.7/ref/settings/*).

This leads to a common question in the Django community: how should the project manage different settings for development, staging, and production environments? Django's wiki (*https://code.djangoproject.com/wiki/SplitSettings*) contains a long list of approaches, and there are a number of reusable applications that aim to tackle this problem. A comparison of those applications can be found on Django Packages (*https://www.djangopackages.com/grids/g/configuration/*). While many of these options can be ideal in some cases, such as converting the *settings.py* into a package and creating modules for each environment, they do not line up well with our example's current single-file setup.

The Twelve Factor App (*http://12factor.net/*) is a methodology for building and deploying HTTP service applications. This methodology recommends separating configuration and code as well as storing configurations in environment variables. This makes the configuration easy to change on the deployment and makes the configuration OS-agnostic.

Let's apply this methodology to our *hello.py* example. There are only two settings that are likely to change between environments: DEBUG and SECRET_KEY.

```
import os
import sys

from django.conf import settings

DEBUG = os.environ.get('DEBUG', 'on') == 'on'

SECRET_KEY = os.environ.get('SECRET_KEY', os.urandom(32))

settings.configure(
    DEBUG=DEBUG,
    SECRET_KEY=SECRET_KEY,
    ROOT_URLCONF=__name__,
    MIDDLEWARE_CLASSES=(
        'django.middleware.common.CommonMiddleware',
        'django.middleware.csrf.CsrfViewMiddleware',
        'django.middleware.clickjacking.XFrameOptionsMiddleware',
    ),
)
```

As you may notice, the default for DEBUG is True, and the SECRET_KEY will be randomly generated each time the application is loaded if it is not set. That will work for this toy example, but if the application were using a piece of Django that requires the SECRET_KEY to remain stable, such as the signed cookies, this would cause the sessions to be frequently invalidated.

Let's examine how this translates to launching the application. To disable the DEBUG setting, we need to set the DEBUG environment variable to something other than on. In a UNIX-derivative system, such as Linux, OS X, or FreeBSD, environment variables are set on the command line with the export command. On Windows, you'd use set.

```
hostname $ export DEBUG=off
hostname $ python hello.py runserver
CommandError: You must set settings.ALLOWED_HOSTS if DEBUG is False.
```

As you can see from the error, the ALLOWED_HOSTS setting isn't configured by our application. ALLOWED_HOSTS is used to validate incoming HTTP HOST header values and should be set to a list of acceptable values for the HOST. If the application is meant to serve example.com, then ALLOWED_HOSTS should allow only for clients that are requesting example.com. If the ALLOWED_HOSTS environment variable isn't set, then it will allow requests only for localhost. This snippet from *hello.py* illustrates.

```
import os
import sys

from django.conf import settings
```

```
DEBUG = os.environ.get('DEBUG', 'on') == 'on'

SECRET_KEY = os.environ.get('SECRET_KEY', os.urandom(32))

ALLOWED_HOSTS = os.environ.get('ALLOWED_HOSTS', 'localhost').split(',')

settings.configure(
    DEBUG=DEBUG,
    SECRET_KEY=SECRET_KEY,
    ALLOWED_HOSTS=ALLOWED_HOSTS,
    ROOT_URLCONF=__name__,
    MIDDLEWARE_CLASSES=(
        'django.middleware.common.CommonMiddleware',
        'django.middleware.csrf.CsrfViewMiddleware',
        'django.middleware.clickjacking.XFrameOptionsMiddleware',
    ),
)
```

With our `ALLOWED_HOSTS` variable set, we now have validation for our incoming HTTP HOST header values.

 For a complete reference on the `ALLOWED_HOSTS` setting, see the official Django documentation (*https://docs.djangoproject.com/en/1.7/ref/settings/#allowed-hosts*).

Outside the development environment, the application might need to serve multiple hosts, such as `localhost` and `example.com`, so the configuration allows us to specify multiple hostnames separated by commas.

```
hostname $ export DEBUG=off
hostname $ export ALLOWED_HOSTS=localhost,example.com
hostname $ python hello.py runserver
...
[06/Aug/2014 19:45:53] "GET / HTTP/1.1" 200 11
```

This gives us a flexible means of configuration across environments. While it would be slightly more difficult to change more complex settings, such as `INSTALLED_APPS` or `MIDDLEWARE_CLASSES`, that is in line with the overall methodology, which encourages minimal differences between environments.

 If you want to make complex changes between environments, you should take time to consider what impact that will have on the testability and deployment of the application.

We can reset DEBUG to the default by removing the environment variable from the shell or by starting a new shell.

```
hostname $ unset DEBUG
```

Reusable Template

So far this example has centered on rethinking the layout created by Django's startproject command. However, this command also allows for using a template to provide the layout. It isn't difficult to transform this file into a reusable template to start future projects using the same base layout.

A template for startproject is a directory or zip file that is rendered as a Django template when the command is run. By default, all of the Python source files will be rendered as a template. The rendering is passed project_name, project_directory, secret_key, and docs_version as the context. The names of the files will also be rendered with this context. To transform *hello.py* into a project template (*project_name/project_name.py*), the relevant parts of the file need to be replaced by these variables.

```
import os
import sys

from django.conf import settings

DEBUG = os.environ.get('DEBUG', 'on') == 'on'

SECRET_KEY = os.environ.get('SECRET_KEY', '{{ secret_key }}')

ALLOWED_HOSTS = os.environ.get('ALLOWED_HOSTS', 'localhost').split(',')

settings.configure(
    DEBUG=DEBUG,
    SECRET_KEY=SECRET_KEY,
    ALLOWED_HOSTS=ALLOWED_HOSTS,
    ROOT_URLCONF=__name__,
    MIDDLEWARE_CLASSES=(
        'django.middleware.common.CommonMiddleware',
        'django.middleware.csrf.CsrfViewMiddleware',
        'django.middleware.clickjacking.XFrameOptionsMiddleware',
    ),
)

from django.conf.urls import url
from django.core.wsgi import get_wsgi_application
from django.http import HttpResponse


def index(request):
    return HttpResponse('Hello World')
```

```
urlpatterns = (
    url(r'^$', index),
)


application = get_wsgi_application()


if __name__ == "__main__":
    from django.core.management import execute_from_command_line

    execute_from_command_line(sys.argv)
```

Now let's save this file as *project_name.py* in a directory called *project_name*. Also, rather than using `os.urandom` for the `SECRET_KEY` default, this code will generate a random secret to be the default each time a new project is created. This makes the `SECRET_KEY` default stable at the project level while still being sufficiently random across projects.

To use the template with `startproject`, you can use the `--template` argument.

hostname $ **django-admin.py startproject foo --template=project_name**

This should create a *foo.py* inside a *foo* directory, which is now ready to run just like the original *hello.py*.

As outlined in this example, it is certainly possible to write and run a Django project without having to use the `startproject` command. The default settings and layout used by Django aren't appropriate for every project. The `--template` option for `startproject` can be used to either expand on these defaults or to trim them down, as you've seen in this chapter.

As with any Python project, there comes a point where organizing the code into multiple modules is an important part of the process. For a sufficiently focused site, with only a handful of URLs, our "Hello World" example may be a reasonable approach.

What is also interesting about this approach is that it isn't immediately obvious that Django has a templating engine or an object-relational mapper (ORM) built in. It is clear that you are free to choose whatever Python libraries you think best solve your problem. You no longer have to use the Django ORM, as the official tutorial might imply. Instead, you get to use the ORM if you want. The project in the next chapter will expand on this single-file example to provide a simple HTTP service and make use of more of the utilities that come with Django.

CHAPTER 2

Stateless Web Application

Most Django applications and tutorials center on some variety of user-generated content, such as to-do lists, blogs, and content management systems. This isn't surprising given Django's original roots in journalism.

In 2005, Django was originally developed at World Online in Lawrence, Kansas, as a way for reporters to quickly create content for the Web. Since then, it has been used by publishing organizations such as *the Washington Post (http://www.washington post.com/), the Guardian (http://www.theguardian.com/), PolitiFact (http://www.politi fact.com/)*, and *the Onion (http://www.theonion.com/)*. This aspect of Django may give the impression that its main purpose is content publishing, or that Django itself is a content management system. With large organizations such as NASA adopting Django as their framework of choice, however, Django has obviously outgrown its original purpose.

In the previous chapter we created a minimal project that made use only of Django's core HTTP handling and URL routing. In this chapter we will expand upon that example to create a stateless web application that uses more of Django's utilities, such as input validation, caching, and templates.

Why Stateless?

HTTP itself is a *stateless* protocol, meaning each request that comes to the server is independent of the previous request. If a particular state is needed, it has to be added at the application layer. Frameworks like Django use cookies and other mechanisms to tie together requests made by the same client.

Along with a persistent session store on the server, the application can then handle tasks, such as holding user authentication across requests. With that comes a number of challenges, as this consistent state reads, and potentially writes, on every request in a distributed server architecture.

As you can imagine, a stateless application does not maintain this consistent state on a server. If authentication or other user credentials are required, then they must be passed by the client on every request. This often makes scaling, caching, and load balancing with stateless applications much easier. You can also make stateless applications easily linkable because the URL can convey most of these states. There are two options we can take, which we'll outline in the next section: reusable apps and composable services.

Reusable Apps Versus Composable Services

Much of the focus in the Django community is about building reusable applications that can be installed and configured into any Django project. However, large applications with different components often have a fairly complex architectural structure.

An approach to combat this complexity is to break large websites into composable services—that is, smaller services that communicate with one another. This doesn't mean that they can't and won't share code at some point. It does mean, however, that each service can then be configured and built separately.

Stateless components, such as REST APIs, are great candidates for breaking out into separate Django projects that can be deployed and tuned independently. Let's build on our Chapter 1 project by creating a placeholder image server using the two techniques just described with Django.

Placeholder Image Server

Placeholder images are frequently used in application prototypes, example projects, or testing environments. A typical placeholder image service will take a URL that indicates the size of the image and generate that image. The URL may contain additional information, such as the color of the image or text to display within the image. Since everything that is needed to construct the requested image is contained within the URL, and there's little need for authentication, this makes a good candidate for a stateless application.

Start by creating a new project called `placeholder` with the `startproject` using the `project_name` template created in Chapter 1.

```
hostname $ django-admin.py startproject placeholder --template=project_name
```

This will generate a *placeholder.py* file for us to begin building our service. If you have used the project template correctly, *placeholder.py* should look like this:

```
import os
import sys

from django.conf import settings

DEBUG = os.environ.get('DEBUG', 'on') == 'on'
```

```python
SECRET_KEY = os.environ.get('SECRET_KEY',
    '%jv_4#hoaqwig2gu!eg#^ozptd*a@88u(aasv7z!7xt^5(*i&k')

ALLOWED_HOSTS = os.environ.get('ALLOWED_HOSTS', 'localhost').split(',')

settings.configure(
    DEBUG=DEBUG,
    SECRET_KEY=SECRET_KEY,
    ALLOWED_HOSTS=ALLOWED_HOSTS,
    ROOT_URLCONF=__name__,
    MIDDLEWARE_CLASSES=(
        'django.middleware.common.CommonMiddleware',
        'django.middleware.csrf.CsrfViewMiddleware',
        'django.middleware.clickjacking.XFrameOptionsMiddleware',
    ),
)

from django.conf.urls import url
from django.core.wsgi import get_wsgi_application
from django.http import HttpResponse


def index(request):
    return HttpResponse('Hello World')


urlpatterns = (
    url(r'^$', index),
)


application = get_wsgi_application()


if __name__ == "__main__":
    from django.core.management import execute_from_command_line

    execute_from_command_line(sys.argv)
```

> The SECRET_KEY setting will be different from this published version, as it is randomly generated by the startproject command.

With our initial settings in place, we can now begin to write our views and start building out the pages to create these responses.

Views

Since this application will be simple, we will need only two views to generate our responses. The first view will render the placeholder images based on their requested width and height. The other view will render the home page content, which explains how the project works and renders a few example images. Because we used Django's `--template` flag when running the `startproject` command, the `index` has already been generated (as shown in this snippet from *placeholder.py*) and will need to be adapted later.

```
...
def placeholder(request, width, height):
    # TODO: Rest of the view will go here
    return HttpResponse('Ok')


def index(request):
    return HttpResponse('Hello World')
...
```

With these simple views in place, we should now think about the URL structure for displaying our placeholders.

URL Patterns

When opening your generated *placeholder.py* file, you'll notice that there is a URL pattern for the server root. We'll also need a route to the `placeholder` view we just created.

The stub of the `placeholder` view will take two arguments: `width` and `height`. As mentioned previously, those parameters will be captured by the URL and passed to the view. Since they will only ever be integers, we'll want to make sure to enforce them by the URL. Since URL patterns in Django use regular expressions to match the incoming URL, we'll be able to easily pass in those parameters.

Captured pattern groups are passed to the view as positional arguments, and named groups are passed as keyword arguments. Named groups are captured using the `?P` syntax, and any digit characters are matched by using `[0-9]`.

This snippet from *placeholder.py* shows how your URL patterns will be laid out to generate those values:

```
...
urlpatterns = (
    url(r'^image/(?P<width>[0-9]+)x(?P<height>[0-9]+)/$', placeholder,
        name='placeholder'),
    url(r'^$', index, name='homepage'),
)
...
```

With these patterns in place, incoming requests to the URL /image/30x25/ will be routed to the `placeholder` view and pass in those values (e.g., `width=30` and `height=25`). Along with the new route for the `placeholder` view, the name `homepage` has been added to the index router. We will also see how naming these URL patterns, while a good practice in general, will be especially useful when we begin to build the templates later.

Placeholder View

Along with the original HTTP request, the placeholder view should accept two integer arguments for the image's height and width values. Though the regular expression will ensure that the height and width consist of digits, they will be passed to the view as strings. The view will need to convert them and may also want to validate that they are a manageable size. We can easily do this by validating user input with Django forms.

Typically forms are used to validate POST and GET content, but they can also be used to validate particular values from the URL, or those stored in cookies. Here is an example from *placeholder.py* of a simple form to validate the height and width of an image:

```
...
from django import forms
from django.conf.urls import url
...

class ImageForm(forms.Form):
    """Form to validate requested placeholder image."""

    height = forms.IntegerField(min_value=1, max_value=2000)
    width = forms.IntegerField(min_value=1, max_value=2000)


def placeholder(request, width, height):
    ...
```

As you can see, the first thing the view should do is validate the requested image size. If the form is valid, then the height and width can be accessed in the form's `cleaned_data` attribute. At this point, the height and width will be converted to integers, and the view can be sure that the values are between 1 and 2000. We'll also need to add validation to the form to send an error message if the values are incorrect, as shown in this excerpt from *placeholder.py*.

```
...
from django import forms
from django.conf.urls import url
from django.core.wsgi import get_wsgi_application
from django.http import HttpResponse, HttpResponseBadRequest


class ImageForm(forms.Form):
    """Form to validate requested placeholder image."""
```

```
        height = forms.IntegerField(min_value=1, max_value=2000)
        width = forms.IntegerField(min_value=1, max_value=2000)


    def placeholder(request, width, height):
        form = ImageForm({'height': height, 'width': width})
        if form.is_valid():
            height = form.cleaned_data['height']
            width = form.cleaned_data['width']
            # TODO: Generate image of requested size
            return HttpResponse('Ok')
        else:
            return HttpResponseBadRequest('Invalid Image Request')
    ...
```

If the form isn't valid, the view will send an error response to the client. Here the view returns an HttpResponseBadRequest, which is a subclass of HttpResponse, and sends a 400 Bad Request response.

Image Manipulation

The view now has the ability to accept and clean the height and width requested by the client, but it does not yet generate the actual image. To handle image manipulation in Python, you need to have Pillow installed as follows:

```
hostname $ pip install Pillow
```

 By default, the install will try to compile Pillow from the source. If you do not have a compiler installed for your environment, or you are missing the necessary headers, it can fail to install. For installation notes on various platforms, visit *https://pillow.readthedocs.org/en/latest/installation.html*.

Creating an image with Pillow requires two arguments: the color mode and the size as a tuple. This view from *placeholder.py* will use the RGB mode and the size from the form's cleaned data values. There is a third argument, which is not required, that sets the color of the image. By default in Pillow, every pixel of the image will be black.

```
    ...
    from io import BytesIO                                          ❶
    from PIL import Image                                           ❷
    ...


    class ImageForm(forms.Form):
        """Form to validate requested placeholder image."""

        height = forms.IntegerField(min_value=1, max_value=2000)
        width = forms.IntegerField(min_value=1, max_value=2000)
```

```
        def generate(self, image_format='PNG'):                         ❸
            """Generate an image of the given type and return as raw bytes."""
            height = self.cleaned_data['height']
            width = self.cleaned_data['width']
            image = Image.new('RGB', (width, height))                    ❹
            content = BytesIO()
            image.save(content, image_format)
            content.seek(0)
            return content


    def placeholder(request, width, height):
        form = ImageForm({'height': height, 'width': width})
        if form.is_valid():
            image = form.generate()                                     ❺
            return HttpResponse(image, content_type='image/png')
        else:
            return HttpResponseBadRequest('Invalid Image Request')
    ...
```

❸ A new `generate` method has been added to the `ImageForm` to encapsulate the logic of building the image. It takes one argument for the image format, which defaults to `PNG`, and returns the image contents as bytes.

❷❹ Using the width and height given by the URL and validated by the form, a new image is constructed using the `Image` class from `Pillow`.

❶❺ The view calls `form.generate` to get the constructed image, and the bytes for the image are then used to construct the response body.

The form then validates the size to prevent requesting too large of an image and consuming too many resources on the server. Once the image has been validated, the view successfully returns the PNG image for the requested width and height. The image content is sent to the client without writing it to the disk.

However, an all-black image, with no sizing information, is not a very stylish or useful placeholder. With `Pillow` we can add this text to the image using the `ImageDraw` module, as shown in this snippet from *placeholder.py*.

```
    ...
    from PIL import Image, ImageDraw                                     ❶
    ...

    class ImageForm(forms.Form):
        ...
        def generate(self, image_format='PNG'):
            """Generate an image of the given type and return as raw bytes."""
            height = self.cleaned_data['height']
            width = self.cleaned_data['width']
            image = Image.new('RGB', (width, height))
```

```
        draw = ImageDraw.Draw(image)                                    ❷
        text = '{} X {}'.format(width, height)
        textwidth, textheight = draw.textsize(text)
        if textwidth < width and textheight < height:
            texttop = (height - textheight) // 2
            textleft = (width - textwidth) // 2
            draw.text((textleft, texttop), text, fill=(255, 255, 255))
        content = BytesIO()
        image.save(content, image_format)
        content.seek(0)
        return content
    ...
```

❶ ❷ generate now uses ImageDraw to add a text overlay if it will fit.

Using ImageDraw, the form uses the current image to create text showing the width and height on the image,

Now that we have our valid placeholder image in place, let's add some caching to help minimize requests to the server.

Adding Caching

The placeholder image view currently regenerates the image and serves it each time the view is requested. Since the width and height of the image are set via the original, we are constantly making unnecessary requests to our server.

One way to avoid this repetition is to use caching. There are two options to think about when you're determining how to utilize caching for this service: server-side and client-side. For server-side caching, you can easily use Django's cache utilities. This will trade memory usage to store the cached values while saving the CPU cycles required to generate the images, as shown in this excerpt from *placeholder.py*.

```
...
from django.conf.urls import url
from django.core.cache import cache                                     ❶
...
class ImageForm(forms.Form):
...
    def generate(self, image_format='PNG'):
        """Generate an image of the given type and return as raw bytes."""
        height = self.cleaned_data['height']
        width = self.cleaned_data['width']
        key = '{}.{}.{}'.format(width, height, image_format)            ❷
        content = cache.get(key)                                        ❸
        if content is None:
            image = Image.new('RGB', (width, height))
            draw = ImageDraw.Draw(image)
            text = '{} X {}'.format(width, height)
            textwidth, textheight = draw.textsize(text)
```

```
            if textwidth < width and textheight < height:
                texttop = (height - textheight) // 2
                textleft = (width - textwidth) // 2
                draw.text((textleft, texttop), text, fill=(255, 255, 255))
            content = BytesIO()
            image.save(content, image_format)
            content.seek(0)
            cache.set(key, content, 60 * 60)                                    ❹
        return content
```

❷ A cache key is generated that depends on the width, height, and image format.

❶ ❸ Before a new image is created, the cache is checked to see if the image is already stored.

❹ When there is a cache miss and a new image is created, the image is cached using the key for an hour.

Django defaults to using a process-local, in-memory cache, but you could use a different backend—such as Memcached or the file system—by configuring the CACHES setting.

A complementary approach is to focus on the client-side behavior and make use of the browser's built-in caching. Django includes an etag decorator for generating and using the ETag headers for the view. The decorator takes a single argument, which is a function to generate the ETag header from the request and view arguments. Here is an example from *placeholder.py* of how we would add that to our view:

```
import hashlib                                                              ❶
import os
...
from django.http import HttpResponse, HttpResponseBadRequest
from django.views.decorators.http import etag                              ❷
...

def generate_etag(request, width, height):                                 ❸
    content = 'Placeholder: {0} x {1}'.format(width, height)
    return hashlib.sha1(content.encode('utf-8')).hexdigest()


@etag(generate_etag)                                                       ❹
def placeholder(request, width, height):
    ...
```

❶ ❸ generate_etag is a new function that takes the same arguments as the placeholder view. It uses hashlib to return an opaque ETag value, which will vary based on the width and height values.

❷ ❹ The generate_etag function will be passed to the etag decorator on the placeholder view.

With this decorator in place, the server will need to generate the image the first time the browser requests it. On subsequent requests, if the browser makes a request with the matching ETag, the browser will receive a 304 Not Modified response for the image. The browser will use the image from the cache and save bandwidth and time to regenerate the `HttpResponse`.

 This view generates an image based only on the width and height. If other features were added, such as the background color or the image text, then the ETag generation would also need to be updated to take these into account.

The `django.middleware.common.CommonMiddleware`, which is enabled in the `MIDDLEWARE_CLASSES` setting, also has support for generating and using ETags if the `USE_ETAGS` setting is enabled. However, there is a difference between how the middleware and the decorator work. The middleware will calculate the ETag based on the md5 hash of the response content. That requires the view to do all the work to generate the content in order to calculate the hash. The result is the same in that the browser will receive a 304 Not Modified response and the bandwidth will be saved. Using the `etag` decorator has the advantage of calculating the ETag prior to the view being called, which will also save on the processing time and resources.

The following is the completed `placeholder` view for *placeholder.py*, along with the form and decorator functions:

```
...
class ImageForm(forms.Form):
    """Form to validate requested placeholder image."""

    height = forms.IntegerField(min_value=1, max_value=2000)
    width = forms.IntegerField(min_value=1, max_value=2000)

    def generate(self, image_format='PNG'):
        """Generate an image of the given type and return as raw bytes."""
        height = self.cleaned_data['height']
        width = self.cleaned_data['width']
        key = '{}.{}.{}'.format(width, height, image_format)
        content = cache.get(key)
        if content is None:
            image = Image.new('RGB', (width, height))
            draw = ImageDraw.Draw(image)
            text = '{} X {}'.format(width, height)
            textwidth, textheight = draw.textsize(text)
            if textwidth < width and textheight < height:
                texttop = (height - textheight) // 2
                textleft = (width - textwidth) // 2
                draw.text((textleft, texttop), text, fill=(255, 255, 255))
            content = BytesIO()
```

```
            image.save(content, image_format)
            content.seek(0)
            cache.set(key, content, 60 * 60)
        return content


def generate_etag(request, width, height):
    content = 'Placeholder: {0} x {1}'.format(width, height)
    return hashlib.sha1(content.encode('utf-8')).hexdigest()


@etag(generate_etag)
def placeholder(request, width, height):
    form = ImageForm({'height': height, 'width': width})
    if form.is_valid():
        image = form.generate()
        return HttpResponse(image, content_type='image/png')
    else:
        return HttpResponseBadRequest('Invalid Image Request')
...
```

With our placeholder view ready, let's go back and build out our home page view to complete our application.

Creating the Home Page View

The home page will render a basic HTML template to explain how the project works and include some sample images. Up to this point, Django has not been configured to render templates. It also has not been configured to serve static resources, such as JavaScript, CSS, and templates. Let's add the necessary settings to serve those static resources: TEMPLATE_DIRS and STATICFILES_DIRS.

Adding Static and Template Settings

Django's template loader will automatically discover templates and static resources inside the installed apps. Since this project does not include any Django applications, these locations need to be configured with the TEMPLATE_DIRS and STATICFILES_DIRS settings. django.contrib.staticfiles will also need to be added to the IN STALLED_APPS for the {% static %} tag and collectstatic commands to be available.

Here is an example of how your directory structure should look at this point:

```
placeholder/
    placeholder.py
```

The templates and static resources would fit nicely in directories next to *placeholder.py*, as in:

```
placeholder/
    placeholder.py
```

```
templates/
    home.html
static/
    site.css
```

To avoid hardcoding these paths, we'll be constructing them relative to the *placehold-er.py* file using the os module from the Python standard library.

```python
import hashlib
import os
import sys

from django.conf import settings

DEBUG = os.environ.get('DEBUG', 'on') == 'on'

SECRET_KEY = os.environ.get('SECRET_KEY',
    '%jv_4#hoaqwig2gu!eg#^ozptd*a@88u(aasv7z!7xt^5(*i&k')

BASE_DIR = os.path.dirname(__file__)

settings.configure(
    DEBUG=DEBUG,
    SECRET_KEY=SECRET_KEY,
    ROOT_URLCONF=__name__,
    MIDDLEWARE_CLASSES=(
        'django.middleware.common.CommonMiddleware',
        'django.middleware.csrf.CsrfViewMiddleware',
        'django.middleware.clickjacking.XFrameOptionsMiddleware',
    ),
    INSTALLED_APPS=(
        'django.contrib.staticfiles',
    ),
    TEMPLATE_DIRS=(
        os.path.join(BASE_DIR, 'templates'),
    ),
    STATICFILES_DIRS=(
        os.path.join(BASE_DIR, 'static'),
    ),
    STATIC_URL='/static/',

    ...
```

Now let's add a simple template structure to finish out this example project with a clean frontend interface.

Home Page Template and CSS

The purpose of the home page for this application is to demonstrate how to use the placeholder images with some brief documentation and examples. It should be saved as *templates/home.html* next to *placeholder.py*. We'll also add in the src reference to our placeholder route to request those images.

```
{% load staticfiles %}
<!DOCTYPE html>
<html lang="en">
<head>
    <meta charset="utf-8">
    <title>Django Placeholder Images</title>
    <link rel="stylesheet" href="{% static 'site.css' %}" type="text/css">
</head>
<body>
    <h1>Django Placeholder Images</h1>
    <p>This server can be used for serving placeholder
    images for any web page.</p>
    <p>To request a placeholder image of a given width and height
    simply include an image with the source pointing to
    <b>/placeholder/&lt;width&gt;x&lt;height&gt;/</b>
    on this server such as:</p>
    <pre>
        &lt;img src="{{ example }}" &gt;
    </pre>
    <h2>Examples</h2>
    <ul>
        <li><img src="{% url 'placeholder' width=50 height=50 %}"></li>
        <li><img src="{% url 'placeholder' width=100 height=50 %}"></li>
        <li><img src="{% url 'placeholder' width=50 height=100 %}"></li>
    <ul>
</body>
</html>
```

Here are some simple styles to add to *site.css* to help create a clean layout. Also, don't forget to save this file in your *static/* folder, as previously outlined in your STATICFILES_DIRS setting:

```
body {
    text-align: center;
}

ul {
    list-type: none;
}

li {
    display: inline-block;
}
```

You should save this as *static/site.css* next to *placeholder.py*, as outlined in the previous section. Finally, we need to update the index view in placeholder.py to render this template:

```python
...
from django.core.cache import cache
from django.core.urlresolvers import reverse                          ❶
from django.core.wsgi import get_wsgi_application
from django.http import HttpResponse, HttpResponseBadRequest          ❷
from django.shortcuts import render
from django.views.decorators.http import etag
...
def index(request):
    example = reverse('placeholder', kwargs={'width': 50, 'height':50})  ❸
    context = {
        'example': request.build_absolute_uri(example)
    }
    return render(request, 'home.html', context)                        ❹
...
```

❶❸ The updated index view builds an example URL by reversing the `placeholder` view, and passes it to the template context.

❷❹ The *home.html* template is rendered using the `render` shortcut.

Completed Project

Now you should have a completed *placeholder.py* file that looks similar to the following one. Along with *home.html* and *site.css* from the previous section, it completes our simple placeholder image service using Django:

```python
import hashlib
import os
import sys

from io import BytesIO
from PIL import Image, ImageDraw

from django.conf import settings

DEBUG = os.environ.get('DEBUG', 'on') == 'on'

SECRET_KEY = os.environ.get('SECRET_KEY',
    '%jv_4#hoaqwig2gu!eg#^ozptd*a@88u(aasv7z!7xt^5(*i&k')

ALLOWED_HOSTS = os.environ.get('ALLOWED_HOSTS', 'localhost').split(',')

BASE_DIR = os.path.dirname(__file__)

settings.configure(
    DEBUG=DEBUG,
```

```
        SECRET_KEY=SECRET_KEY,
        ALLOWED_HOSTS=ALLOWED_HOSTS,
        ROOT_URLCONF=__name__,
        MIDDLEWARE_CLASSES=(
            'django.middleware.common.CommonMiddleware',
            'django.middleware.csrf.CsrfViewMiddleware',
            'django.middleware.clickjacking.XFrameOptionsMiddleware',
        ),
        INSTALLED_APPS=(
            'django.contrib.staticfiles',
        ),
        TEMPLATE_DIRS=(
            os.path.join(BASE_DIR, 'templates'),
        ),
        STATICFILES_DIRS=(
            os.path.join(BASE_DIR, 'static'),
        ),
        STATIC_URL='/static/',
)

from django import forms
from django.conf.urls import url
from django.core.cache import cache
from django.core.urlresolvers import reverse
from django.core.wsgi import get_wsgi_application
from django.http import HttpResponse, HttpResponseBadRequest
from django.shortcuts import render
from django.views.decorators.http import etag


class ImageForm(forms.Form):
    """Form to validate requested placeholder image."""

    height = forms.IntegerField(min_value=1, max_value=2000)
    width = forms.IntegerField(min_value=1, max_value=2000)

    def generate(self, image_format='PNG'):
        """Generate an image of the given type and return as raw bytes."""
        height = self.cleaned_data['height']
        width = self.cleaned_data['width']
        key = '{}.{}.{}'.format(width, height, image_format)
        content = cache.get(key)
        if content is None:
            image = Image.new('RGB', (width, height))
            draw = ImageDraw.Draw(image)
            text = '{} X {}'.format(width, height)
            textwidth, textheight = draw.textsize(text)
            if textwidth < width and textheight < height:
                texttop = (height - textheight) // 2
                textleft = (width - textwidth) // 2
                draw.text((textleft, texttop), text, fill=(255, 255, 255))
            content = BytesIO()
```

```python
            image.save(content, image_format)
            content.seek(0)
            cache.set(key, content, 60 * 60)
        return content


def generate_etag(request, width, height):
    content = 'Placeholder: {0} x {1}'.format(width, height)
    return hashlib.sha1(content.encode('utf-8')).hexdigest()


@etag(generate_etag)
def placeholder(request, width, height):
    form = ImageForm({'height': height, 'width': width})
    if form.is_valid():
        image = form.generate()
        return HttpResponse(image, content_type='image/png')
    else:
        return HttpResponseBadRequest('Invalid Image Request')


def index(request):
    example = reverse('placeholder', kwargs={'width': 50, 'height':50})
    context = {
        'example': request.build_absolute_uri(example)
    }
    return render(request, 'home.html', context)


urlpatterns = (
    url(r'^image/(?P<width>[0-9]+)x(?P<height>[0-9]+)/$', placeholder,
        name='placeholder'),
    url(r'^$', index, name='homepage'),
)


application = get_wsgi_application()


if __name__ == "__main__":
    from django.core.management import execute_from_command_line

    execute_from_command_line(sys.argv)
```

Now let's go ahead and use `runserver` to view our new placeholder image service.

```
hostname $ python placeholder.py runserver
```

You should see the screen shown in Figure 2-1.

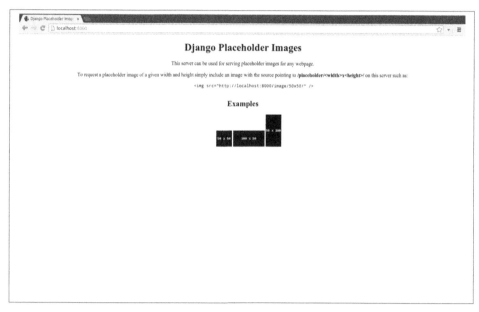

Figure 2-1. Placeholder image screenshot

If you are getting a 404 error for the *site.css*, check that you are running with DEBUG enabled. Django's development server does not serve the static resources when DEBUG is False. You may need to unset the DEBUG environment variable, as shown in the previous chapter.

This project is no longer just a toy "Hello World" example. This is a fully functional web application built with Django and shows how you can do something fairly complex with Django in a very lightweight way. It makes use of not just the HTTP utilities provided by Django but also the built-in input validations, caching, templating, and static file management. In the next chapter, we'll focus on creating another lightweight example by building a static site generator using Django.

CHAPTER 3

Building a Static Site Generator

Django is known as the framework "for perfectionists with deadlines" for a reason. As we mentioned in Chapter 2, it was originally created in a newsroom setting so that journalists could rapidly produce, edit, and publish news stories on the fly. Since its open source release in July 2005, Django has been used by web developers to rapidly create websites and applications at varying scale. At the time, it was the first of its kind, and it has since grown to be a front-runner for web development. We now see it used everywhere from personal to large-scale applications such as Pinterest and Instagram.

While choosing the best framework is an important part of starting any project, deciding on the proper workflow is also a priority. Designers and developers being able to work effectively side by side is crucial to creating a successful end product. Yet how efficient is Django when designers and developers collaborate with one another?

One way we have found that designers and developers work best is for them to begin the project in parallel. Both parties are able to hit the ground running and utilize the portions of the framework they need to get started. A beneficial tutorial for achieving this goal is to create a static site application within our Django projects.

Creating Static Sites with Django

Most static site examples involve the creation of a blogging site, like Jekyll or Hyde. These generally include a simple set of base templates, URL patterns, and file architecture to serve up each static page. However, even with its original intention to work in a fast-paced environment, Django is not a web framework most developers think of using to create static websites. In this chapter, we'll walk you through the steps to create a rapid prototyping site with Django to help us quickly generate websites and applications.

What Is Rapid Prototyping?

Process is a very important part of a project when you're creating web applications on a large team. Yet it can easily become heavily loaded with unnecessary steps to reach the final product. The rapid prototyping workflow is a way to bypass those steps and reach your end goal more efficiently. This principle goes hand in hand with the primary purpose for which Django was created.

In his talk "Death to Wireframes, Long Live Rapid Prototyping," Bermon Painter stated that there are five steps to the rapid prototyping process:

1. **Observe and analyze.** This is the part of the process where you figure out your end-user goals. It is all about brainstorming with your teammates about what you want to build (e.g., Who are your users? What will each user want from your product?).

2. **Build.** Using HTML, CSS, and JavaScript, the team now works together to create a *minimum viable product* (MVP) using only gray box samples and simple layouts.

3. **Ship.** Create a seamless way for every single person who touches the code on your team to deploy and ship code for viewing and/or testing purposes.

4. **Adopt and educate.** Teach your users how to use the new features or design of your project, and listen to their feedback.

5. **Iterate and maintain.** Take your users' feedback and iterate back through the rapid prototyping process. This helps refine your end product to create an even more successful result. Also, maintain the code you are working on by staying up to date with any new package releases.

Where and how does Django fit into the workflow of rapid prototyping? Throughout the rest of this chapter, we'll step you through how to implement the Build and Ship portions of the rapid prototyping process on a Django project by creating static content. We'll be building out a generic website to help you understand the process of creating a static site as a rapid prototyping tool.

Initial Project Layout

As we did with the previous two chapters, we'll be leveraging the single-file method to generate our settings and other components to run our project. We'll also need to create a few other typical Django project files we normally see when using the `startproject` command. Let's begin by generating the initial scaffolding.

File/Folder Scaffolding

There are only a few elements that are required for our rapid prototyping site to run: views, URLs, and templates. Let's start by creating a basic file structure for our site. We'll create a folder called *sitebuilder* and place our *init.py*, *views.py*, *urls.py*, and *templates* folders inside that folder.

We'll also need to add a *static* folder at the root level of the *sitebuilder* folder to hold any images, CSS, or JavaScript we'll need. Let's add empty *js* and *css* folders too, and put them in the *templates* folder.

Based on what we have already learned in the previous two chapters, we'll be leveraging the single-file method to store our settings and other configurations for our application. The settings will be stored in a single *prototypes.py* file. You should now have a set of folders created with the following file structure in place:

```
prototypes.py
sitebuilder
    __init__.py
    static/
        js/
        css/
    templates/
    urls.py
    views.py
```

Now we can start adding some simple settings to get our project up and running.

Basic Settings

As with our file layout, we'll only need to a few settings in order to get things started. Let's add these basic settings into the *prototypes.py* file, as well as add our sitebuilder application into the INSTALLED_APPS setting.

```python
import sys

from django.conf import settings


settings.configure(
    DEBUG=True,
    SECRET_KEY='b0mqvak1p2sqm6p#+8o8fyxf+ox(le)8&jh_5^sxa!=7!+wxj0',
    ROOT_URLCONF='sitebuilder.urls',
    MIDDLEWARE_CLASSES=(),
    INSTALLED_APPS=(
        'django.contrib.staticfiles',
        'django.contrib.webdesign',                                        ❶
        'sitebuilder',
    ),
    STATIC_URL='/static/',
)


if __name__ == "__main__":
    from django.core.management import execute_from_command_line
```

```
execute_from_command_line(sys.argv)
```

 `django.contrib.webdesign` is an application for creating placeholder text in our applications. With this in place, we can seamlessly add placeholder text into our prototypes by using the `{% lorem %}` tag.

 In Django 1.8, `django.contrib.webdesign` will be deprecated and `{% lorem %}` becomes a built-in template tag. This means `django.contrib.webdesign` will be removed as part of the Django 2.0 release.

To complete our initial project layout, we'll need to add in a URL setting in our *urls.py* file. Open up that file (*/sitebuilder/urls.py*) and add the following line to create the initial setup:

```
urlpatterns = ()
```

Now let's try running our application as a quick sanity check to make sure everything is working as it should.

```
hostname $ python prototype.py runserver
Performing system checks...

System check identified no issues (0 silenced).
August 7, 2014 - 10:40:38
Django version 1.7c2, using settings None
Starting development server at http://127.0.0.1:8000/
Quit the server with CONTROL-C.
```

When you visit *http://127.0.0.1:8000* in your browser, you should see the screen shown in Figure 3-1.

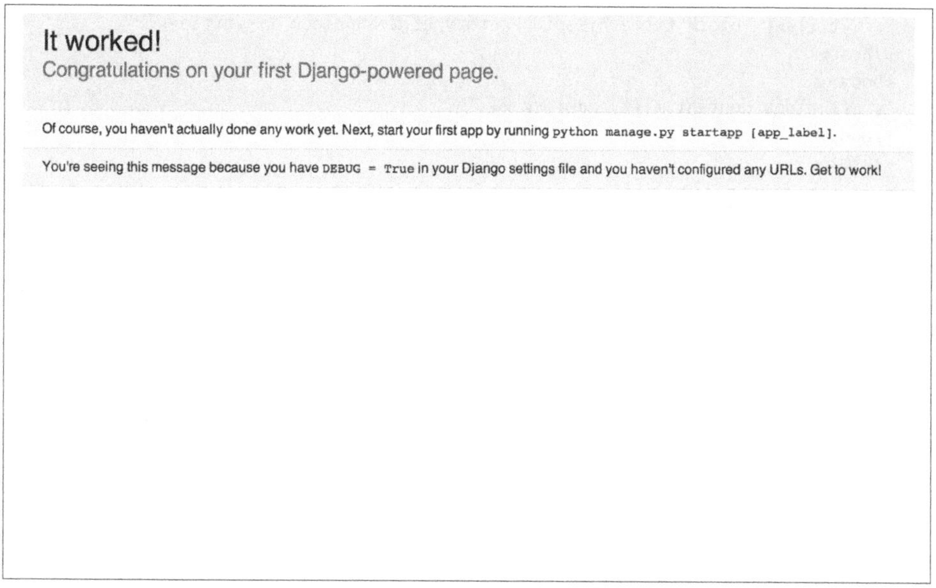

It worked!
Congratulations on your first Django-powered page.

Of course, you haven't actually done any work yet. Next, start your first app by running `python manage.py startapp [app_label]`.

You're seeing this message because you have `DEBUG = True` in your Django settings file and you haven't configured any URLs. Get to work!

Figure 3-1. Initial project screen

With our basic settings in place and our application running, we can begin creating the template structure and page rendering for our prototypes.

Page Rendering

As with most Django projects, creating a solid base template is a crucial part of building out the frontend architecture. Once that foundation is in place, you can begin to structure the rest of your templates.

Creating Our Base Templates

As with other static site generators, there are generally a few base templates that the entire site is built from. They consist of generic layouts that will be utilized throughout the site and create the basic structure for each page. For this application we'll be creating two basic templates: *base.html* and *page.html*.

To begin, let's create our *base.html* file in the *sitebuilder/templates* directory as our base template and add the following layout.

```
<!DOCTYPE html>
<html lang="en">
<head>
    <meta charset="utf-8">
    <meta http-equiv="X-UA-Compatible" content="IE=edge">
    <meta name="viewport" content="width=device-width,initial-scale=1">
```

```
    <title>{% block title %}Rapid Prototypes{% endblock %}</title>
  </head>
  <body>
    {% block content %}{% endblock %}
  </body>
</html>
```

Since we are creating a statically generated site, we'll need to add Django's static files tag to our template. Let's also create a blank CSS file named *site.css*, which we'll leverage later, and place it into our *static/css* folder.

```
hostname $ touch sitebuilder/static/css/site.css
```

Now let's add the following new structure to our *base.html* template.

```
{% load staticfiles %}
<!DOCTYPE html>
<html lang="en">
  <head>
    <meta charset="utf-8">
    <meta http-equiv="X-UA-Compatible" content="IE=edge">
    <meta name="viewport" content="width=device-width,initial-scale=1">
    <title>{% block title %}Rapid Prototypes{% endblock %}</title>
    <link rel="stylesheet" href="{% static 'css/site.css' %}">
  </head>
  <body>
    {% block content %}{% endblock %}
  </body>
</html>
```

Since we haven't added any specific URL patterns or views, we'll still see our "It worked!" template (shown in Figure 3-1) when running `python prototypes.py runserver`.

In the next section we'll start building out the views and URLs and add a *page.html* file to build our prototypes with.

Static Page Generator

As with other static site generators, with ours we want to be able to easily create new pages on the fly. To do this, we'll need to add a settings variable to reference our file path, views to render the page, and a lightweight URL structure to point our dynamic pages to.

Let's start by adding a *pages* directory to store all of our prototyped pages:

```
hostname $ mkdir pages
```

This is the directory where all of our prototype templates will live. Now let's add a way for us to reference this folder by using a settings variable in our *prototypes.py* file.

```
import os
import sys
```

```
from django.conf import settings


BASE_DIR = os.path.dirname(__file__)
...
    STATIC_URL='/static/',
    SITE_PAGES_DIRECTORY=os.path.join(BASE_DIR, 'pages'),
...
```

We can now easily access the *pages* folder in which our prototype files live. The final output we want to build will be to produce a site with a URL structure that matches the files in the *pages* directory using the content of each page. The layout of the pages will be determined by the templates defined in the *templates* folder. This will help separate the page content from the page layout.

Before we get to building the static output, we'll need to build out our *views.py* file (within the *sitebuilder* folder) to dynamically render the pages for working on them locally. Let's add a view to render each of the templates created inside our *pages* folder.

```
import os

from django.conf import settings
from django.http import Http404
from django.shortcuts import render
from django.template import Template
from django.utils._os import safe_join


def get_page_or_404(name):
    """Return page content as a Django template or raise 404 error."""
    try:
        file_path = safe_join(settings.SITE_PAGES_DIRECTORY, name)     ❶
    except ValueError:
        raise Http404('Page Not Found')
    else:
        if not os.path.exists(file_path):
            raise Http404('Page Not Found')

    with open(file_path, 'r') as f:                                    ❷
        page = Template(f.read())

    return page


def page(request, slug='index'):
    """Render the requested page if found."""
    file_name = '{}.html'.format(slug)
    page = get_page_or_404(file_name)
    context = {
        'slug': slug,
        'page': page,
```

```
        }
        return render(request, 'page.html', context)                    ❸
```

❶ Uses `safe_join` to join the page's file path with the template's filename and returns a normalized, absolute version of the final path.

❷ Opens up each file and instantiates a new Django template object with its contents.

❸ Passes the `page` and `slug` context to be rendered by the *page.html* layout template.

This project will treat files within this directory as Django templates, but an alternative approach would be to define the page content as Markdown, RestructuredText, or your markup language of choice. An even more flexible approach would be to render the page content based on its extension. We'll leave these improvements as exercises for the reader.

To complete this view, we need to create the *page.html* template (under *sitebuilder/templates*) for our prototype page rendering, remembering that the included context to render is passed as a `page` context variable.

```
{% extends "base.html" %}

{% block title %}{{ block.super}} - {{ slug|capfirst }}{% endblock %}

{% block content %}
    {% include page %}
{% endblock %}
```

With all of our view context in place, we can now build out our *urls.py* file (in the *sitebuilder* folder) to include where to send our request for our listing and detail pages.

```
from django.conf.urls import url

from .views import page


urlpatterns = (
    url(r'^(?P<slug>[\w./-]+)/$', page, name='page'),
    url(r'^$', page, name='homepage'),
)
```

With our base templates in place, we can now start adding whatever content we want to create our static site. The root of the server / will call the `page` view without passing the `slug` argument, meaning it will use the default `index` slug value. To render the home page, let's add a basic *index.html* template to our *pages* folder to test out our application.

```
<h1>Welcome To the Site</h1>
<p>Insert marketing copy here.</p>
```

```
hostname $ python prototype.py runserver
Performing system checks...

System check identified no issues (0 silenced).
August 7, 2014 - 11:40:38
Django version 1.7c2, using settings None
Starting development server at http://127.0.0.1:8000/
Quit the server with CONTROL-C.
```

When you visit *http://127.0.0.1:8000* in your browser, you should see the screen shown in Figure 3-2.

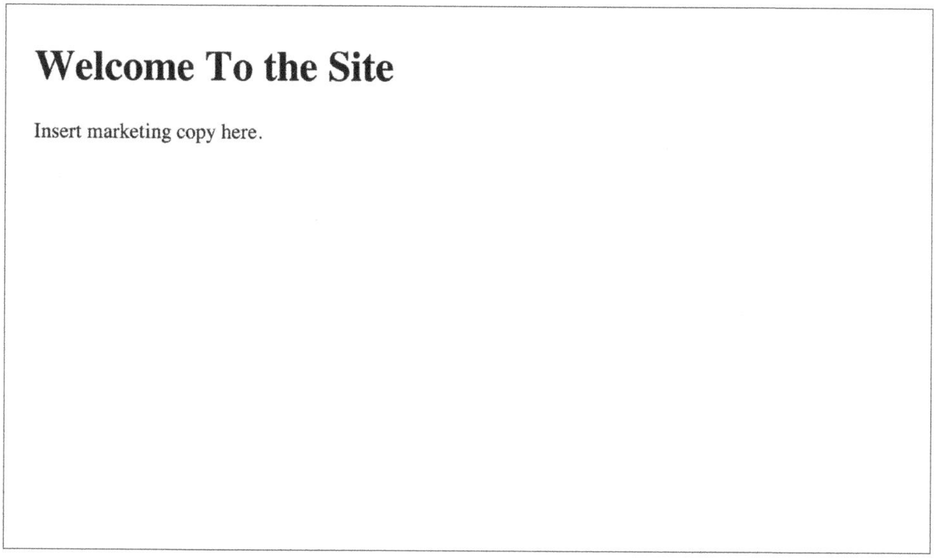

Welcome To the Site

Insert marketing copy here.

Figure 3-2. Welcome page

You can now easily add as many pages as you like to the *pages* folder to help build out the prototypes. In the next section, we'll add some basic styles and layouts as we continue to build out our project.

Basic Styling

As mentioned earlier, this process is meant to get you started in building out your projects. Twitter Bootstrap is a great option to help create an initial styling from which to build. So let's go ahead and download the files we'll need to save to our *static* directory to integrate Twitter Bootstrap into our styles.

Go to the following URL to download the static dependencies to your desktop: *https://github.com/twbs/bootstrap/releases/download/v3.2.0/bootstrap-3.2.0-dist.zip*.   Unzip the files and place each in its proper directory in the *static* folder. Your folder structure should end up looking something like the following:

```
prototypes.py
pages/
sitebuilder
    __init__.py
    static/
        js/
            bootstrap.min.js
        css/
            bootstrap-theme.css.map
            bootstrap-theme.min.css
            bootstrap.css.map
            bootstrap.min.css
            site.css
        fonts/
            glyphicons-halflings-regular.eot
            glyphicons-halflings-regular.svg
            glyphicons-halflings-regular.ttf
            glyphicons-halflings-regular.woff
    templates/
    urls.py
    views.py
```

Since jQuery is a dependency for some of the things we'll be creating throughout this project, we'll need to download that too. Go to *http://cdnjs.cloudflare.com/ajax/libs/jquery/2.1.1/jquery.min.js* and save this version into the *static/js* directory.

We'll now add a reference to these files to our *base.html* template (under *sitebuilder/templates*).

```
{% load staticfiles %}
<!DOCTYPE html>
<html lang="en">
    <head>
        <meta charset="utf-8">
        <meta http-equiv="X-UA-Compatible" content="IE=edge">
        <meta name="viewport" content="width=device-width,initial-scale=1">
        <title>{% block title %}Rapid Prototypes{% endblock %}</title>
        <link rel="stylesheet" href="{% static 'css/bootstrap.min.css' %}">
        <link rel="stylesheet" href="{% static 'css/site.css' %}">
    </head>
    <body>
        {% block content %}{% endblock %}
        <script src="{% static 'js/jquery.min.js' %}"></script>
        <script src="{% static 'js/bootstrap.min.js' %}"></script>
    </body>
</html>
```

Now we can start adding our prototypes with some minimal styling and interactions provided by the CSS and JavaScript that came with Twitter Bootstrap.

Prototype Layouts and Navigation

Typically, when starting to create a website we first think about what will appear on the home page. We'll start this section by building out a simple home page layout, and then we'll build out additional pages with a simple navigation.

We'll also be leveraging Twitter Bootstrap's column-based layout styles and use the 12-column grid that the framework provides. Let's revamp our *index.html* template (in the *pages* folder) and use these styles to create a basic marketing page.

```
{% load webdesign %}
<div class="jumbotron">
    <div class="container">
        <h1>Welcome To the Site</h1>
        <p>Insert marketing copy here.</p>
    </div>
</div>
<div class="container">
    <div class="row">
        <div class="col-md-6">
            <h2>About</h2>
            <p>{% lorem %}</p>
        </div>
        <div class="col-md-6">
            <h2>Contact</h2>
            <p>{% lorem %}</p>
            <p>
                <a class="btn btn-default"
                    href="{% url 'page' 'contact' %}" role="button">
                    Contact us »
                </a>
            </p>
        </div>
    </div>
</div>

<hr>

<footer>
    <div class="container">
        <p>&copy; Your Company {% now 'Y' %}</p>
    </div>
</footer>
```

There are a few things going on here that we want to note. First, we're using our page URL to create URLs to other prototype pages. Now we can create a static site with dynamic links that go to other static pages. We'll get into building those out later in this section. Trying to access them now would raise a 404 Not Found error.

You'll also notice here that we are utilizing Django's {% lorem %} tag to generate place-holder text for our home page. These tags make it easier for us to quickly generate pages even if there is no copy currently available for them.

We'll also need to add some CSS to our *site.css* file (under */sitebuilder/static/css*) to help with the padding around the content. This is a typical practice with Twitter Bootstrap because of its layout structure, and it is usually left to the designer to determine the padding value.

```css
body {
    padding: 50px 0 30px;
}
```

Since we're adding in more pages, let's add some basic navigation to our *base.html* template (under *sitebuilder/templates*) to point to the sitewide navigation.

```
...
<body id="{% block body-id %}body{% endblock %}">
    {% block top-nav-wrapper %}
    <div class="navbar navbar-inverse navbar-fixed-top" role="navigation">
        <div class="container">
            <div class="navbar-header">
                <button type="button" class="navbar-toggle"
                    data-toggle="collapse" data-target=".navbar-collapse">
                    <span class="sr-only">Toggle navigation</span>
                    <span class="icon-bar"></span>
                    <span class="icon-bar"></span>
                    <span class="icon-bar"></span>
                </button>
                <a class="navbar-brand" href="/">Rapid Prototypes</a>
            </div>
            <div class="collapse navbar-collapse">
                <ul class="nav navbar-nav">
                    <li {% if slug == 'index' %}class="active"{% endif %}>
                        <a href="/">Home</a>
                    </li>
                    <li {% if slug == 'contact' %}class="active"{% endif %}>
                        <a href="{% url 'page' 'contact' %}">Contact</a>
                    </li>
                </ul>
                <ul class="nav navbar-nav navbar-right">
                    <li {% if slug == 'login' %}class="active"{% endif %}>
                        <a href="{% url 'page' 'login' %}">Login</a>
                    </li>
                </ul>
            </div>
        </div>
    </div>
    {% endblock %}
    {% block content %}{% endblock %}
...
```

You'll notice that in the <body> tag we've added a {% block body-id %} template tag. This helps with targeting the CSS styles for each portion of the page and is a useful practice. We'll also want to add this to our *page.html* layout in */sitebuilder/templates*. We'll use the page's {{ slug }} value to create a dynamic ID value for each page.

```
{% extends "base.html" %}

{% block title %}{{ block.super }} - {{ slug|capfirst }}{% endblock %}

{% block body-id %}{{ slug|slugify }}{% endblock %} ❶

{% block content %}
    {% include page %}
{% endblock %}
```

❶   Here we've also added the slugify filter to convert any of the slugs generated by our pages to a lowercase value and make consistent ID values.

Let's do a quick check and run our python prototypes.py runserver command again. When you go to *http://127.0.0.1:8000/* in your browser, you should see the screen shown in Figure 3-3.

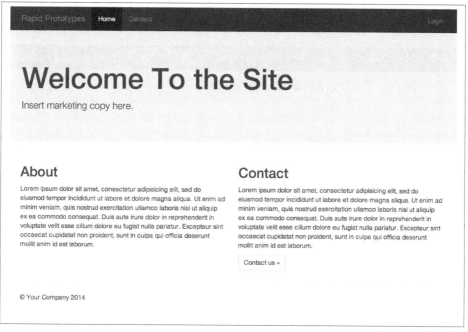

Figure 3-3. Welcome page styled

Now that we have the basic structure in place, let's add a few more templates to link up our contact and login pages as referenced in our *index.html* template. We'll start with our login page first by adding a *login.html* template to our *pages* folder, as seen in Figure 3-4.

```
<div class="container">
    <div class="row">
        <form class="form-signup col-md-6 col-md-offset-3" role="form">
            <h2 class="form-signin-heading">Login to Your Account</h2>
            <div class="form-group">
                <input type="email" class="form-control"
                    placeholder="Email address" required=""
                    autofocus="" autocomplete="off" >
            </div>
            <div class="form-group">
                <input type="password" class="form-control"
                    placeholder="Password" required="" autocomplete="off" >
            </div>
            <div class="form-group">
                <button class="btn btn-lg btn-primary btn-block"
                    type="submit">Login</button>
            </div>
        </form>
    </div>
</div>
```

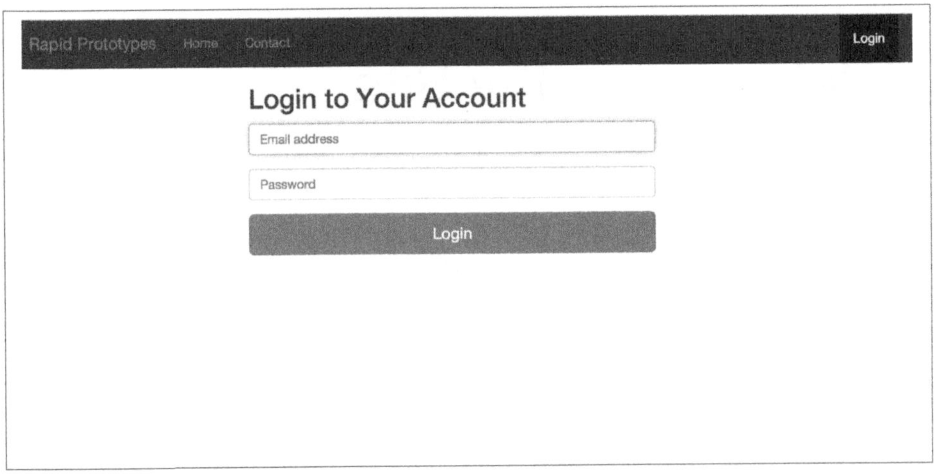

Figure 3-4. Login page

While we have a nicely styled login page, it's not functional yet. This is a prime example of how designers and developers can work in parallel and still perform their portion of the project at their own pace. Now when the login form is ready to be synced with the backend, it already has some context and styling around it. Let's do the same for a generic contact page and add a *contact.html* template in our pages folder, as seen in Figure 3-5.

```html
<div class="container">
    <div class="row">
        <form class="form-contact col-md-6" role="form">
            <h2>Contact Us</h2>
            <div class="form-group">
                <input type="email" class="form-control"
                    placeholder="Email address" required="" >
            </div>
            <div class="form-group">
                <input type="text" class="form-control"
                    placeholder="Title" required="" >
            </div>
            <div class="form-group">
                <textarea class="form-control" required=""
                    placeholder="Your message..." ></textarea>
            </div>
            <div class="form-group">
                <button class="btn btn-lg btn-primary btn-block"
                    type="submit">Submit</button>
            </div>
        </form>
        <div class="col-md-4 col-md-offset-2">
            <h2>Our Office</h2>
            <address>
                <strong>Company Name</strong><br>
                123 Something St<br>
                New York, NY 00000<br>
                (212) 555 - 1234
            </address>
        </div>
    </div>
</div>
```

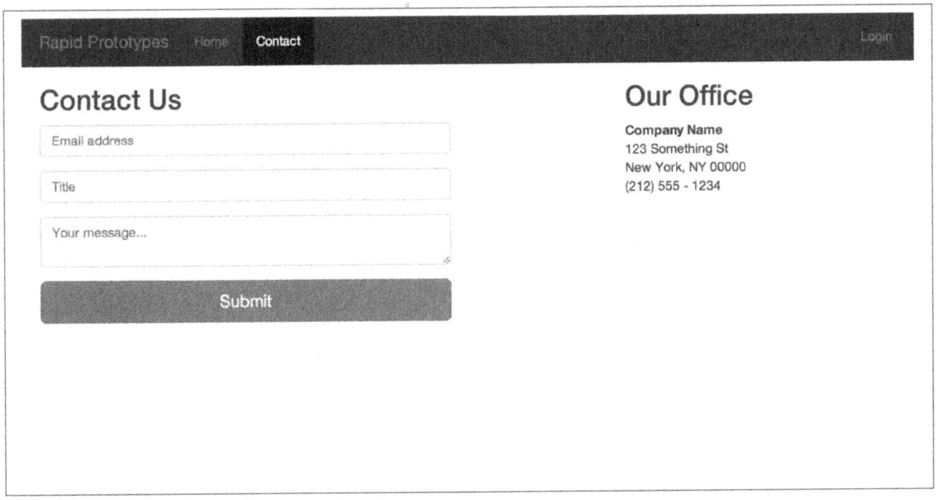

Figure 3-5. Contact us page

Again, while this form is not currently working dynamically, we've generated a simple prototype layout that can easily be synced. This is one of the core concepts of working with rapid prototypes on a project, and illustrates how designers and developers can work together in parallel seamlessly.

In the next section we'll make this dynamic content truly static through a simple management command.

Generating Static Content

While we do have a working prototype application that creates a simple static site, our application is technically not a static site that generates static content yet (e.g., HTML). Let's create a custom management command that outputs that content into a deployable static folder.

Settings Configuration

We'll need to add a few folders inside our *sitebuilder* directory to create our custom management command. We'll also need to add a uniquely named file for our command and add it within this file structure. Our folders should now be organized as follows.

```
prototypes.py
pages/
sitebuilder
    __init__.py
    management/
        __init__.py
        commands/
```

```
            __init__.py
            build.py
    static/
        js/
        css/
        fonts/
    templates/
    urls.py
    views.py
```

Before we begin building out our custom command, we'll need a few new settings for our static output directory to work correctly. Let's start by adding those into our *prototypes.py* file.

```
settings.configure(
...
    STATIC_URL='/static/',
    SITE_PAGES_DIRECTORY=os.path.join(BASE_DIR, 'pages'),
    SITE_OUTPUT_DIRECTORY=os.path.join(BASE_DIR, '_build'),    ❶
    STATIC_ROOT=os.path.join(BASE_DIR, '_build', 'static'),    ❷
)
...
```

❶   This setting configures the output directory where the statically generated files will live once the command has completed.

❷   Here is where we enable static content to live in inside the _build directory.

As with the STATIC_ROOT, the SITE_OUTPUT_DIRECTORY will store generated content and will not be checked into version control. With the settings in place and our folder structure laid out, we can move on to writing our management command.

Custom Management Command

Now we can begin to build our custom management command to generate and output our static site. We'll use the *build.py* file we created in the previous scaffolding (under */sitebuilder/management/commands*) and use the following code structure.

```
import os
import shutil

from django.conf import settings
from django.core.management import call_command
from django.core.management.base import BaseCommand
from django.core.urlresolvers import reverse
from django.test.client import Client


def get_pages():                                                    ❶
    for name in os.listdir(settings.SITE_PAGES_DIRECTORY):
        if name.endswith('.html'):
```

```
        yield name[:-5]


class Command(BaseCommand):
    help = 'Build static site output.'

    def handle(self, *args, **options):
        """Request pages and build output."""
        if os.path.exists(settings.SITE_OUTPUT_DIRECTORY):       ❷
            shutil.rmtree(settings.SITE_OUTPUT_DIRECTORY)
        os.mkdir(settings.SITE_OUTPUT_DIRECTORY)
        os.makedirs(settings.STATIC_ROOT)
        call_command('collectstatic', interactive=False,         ❸
            clear=True, verbosity=0)
        client = Client()
        for page in get_pages():                                 ❹
            url = reverse('page', kwargs={'slug': page})
            response = client.get(url)
            if page == 'index':
                output_dir = settings.SITE_OUTPUT_DIRECTORY
            else:
                output_dir = os.path.join(settings.SITE_OUTPUT_DIRECTORY, page)
                os.makedirs(output_dir)
            with open(os.path.join(output_dir, 'index.html'), 'wb') as f:  ❺
                f.write(response.content)
```

❷ This code checks whether the *output* directory exists, and if so, removes it to create a clean version.

❸ On this line we're utilizing the `call_command` utility to run the `collecstatic` command to copy all of the site static resources into the `STATIC_ROOT`, which is configured to be inside the `SITE_OUTPUT_DIRECTORY`.

❶❹ Here we loop through the *pages* directory and collect all of our *.html* files that are located there.

❺ Here is where our templates are rendered as static content. We're using the Django test client to mimic crawling the site pages and writing the rendered content into the `SITE_OUTPUT_DIRECTORY`.

We should now be able to run our management command to create the *build* directory, which will be generated at the root level of our *projects* directory.

```
hostname $ python prototypes.py build
```

You should now have a *build* directory located at the root level of your project with all of your static files inside. Let's run a simple Python server locally to test our static files.

```
hostname $ cd _build
hostname $ python -m http.server 9000
Serving HTTP on 0.0.0.0 port 9000 ...
```

Now when you go to *0.0.0.0:9000*, you should see the same index page as referenced in Figure 3-3. We can now easily deploy these files to whatever hosting platform we desire and show our rapid prototyping progress.

Building a Single Page

As with any project, there are times when we'll want to edit only a few files in our site. With the current state of our management command, however, we continually rebuild our entire static files directory. Let's configure it to be able to build out one page at a time.

To start, we'll need to add an argument in *build.py* (under */sitebuilder/management/commands/*) to build either a single file or all of the content.

```
...
from django.core.management import call_command
from django.core.management.base import BaseCommand, CommandError        ❶
...
class Command(BaseCommand):
    help = 'Build static site output.'

    def handle(self, *args, **options):
        """Request pages and build output."""
        if args:                                                         ❷
            pages = args
            available = list(get_pages())
            invalid = []
            for page in pages:
                if page not in available:
                    invalid.append(page)
            if invalid:
                msg = 'Invalid pages: {}'.format(', '.join(invalid))
                raise CommandError(msg)                                  ❸
        else:
            pages = get_pages()
            if os.path.exists(settings.SITE_OUTPUT_DIRECTORY):
                shutil.rmtree(settings.SITE_OUTPUT_DIRECTORY)
            os.mkdir(settings.SITE_OUTPUT_DIRECTORY)
            os.makedirs(settings.STATIC_ROOT)
        call_command('collectstatic', interactive=False,
            clear=True, verbosity=0)
        client = Client()
        for page in pages:
            url = reverse('page', kwargs={'slug': page})
            response = client.get(url)
            if page == 'index':
                output_dir = settings.SITE_OUTPUT_DIRECTORY
            else:
                output_dir = os.path.join(settings.SITE_OUTPUT_DIRECTORY, page)
                if not os.path.exists(output_dir):                      ❹
                    os.makedirs(output_dir)
```

```
with open(os.path.join(output_dir, 'index.html'), 'wb') as f:
    f.write(response.content)
```

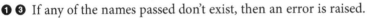 This section adds a check for whether any arguments are passed into the command. More than one name can be passed at a time.

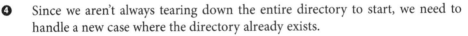 If any of the names passed don't exist, then an error is raised.

❹ Since we aren't always tearing down the entire directory to start, we need to handle a new case where the directory already exists.

Now we can run the following command to compile a single page into static content.

```
hostname $ python prototypes.py build index
```

In the next section, we'll configure our static files even further by using Django's static files and django-compressor.

Serving and Compressing Static Files

As with any page request on the Web, there are various processes that run to render each of our pages. Each request has its own expense and cost to our page load. To combat these time lapses, Django has a built-in caching framework for us to utilize on our web applications.

Creating compressed static files is another way for us to create fast page loads. In this section, we'll explore both hashing and leveraging django-compressor to compress these files and create an even more streamlined process for serving our pages.

Hashing Our CSS and JavaScript Files

Django comes with a few helpful settings for storing and serving images, CSS, and JavaScript files. We'll use one of the settings for creating hashes of our CSS and JavaScript filenames. This is a useful technique for breaking browser caches when the files change. With these names, which are unique based on the file contents, the web server can be configured with Expires headers for the far future for these files.

To start off, we'll add in the necessary setting to our *prototypes.py* file:

```
...
settings.configure(
    DEBUG=True,
    SECRET_KEY='b0mqvak1p2sqm6p#+8o8fyxf+ox(le)8&jh_5^sxa!=7!+wxj0',
    ROOT_URLCONF='sitebuilder.urls',
    MIDDLEWARE_CLASSES=(),
    INSTALLED_APPS=(
        'django.contrib.staticfiles',
        'django.contrib.webdesign',
        'sitebuilder',
    ),
```

```
        STATIC_URL='/static/',
        SITE_PAGES_DIRECTORY=os.path.join(BASE_DIR, 'pages'),
        SITE_OUTPUT_DIRECTORY=os.path.join(BASE_DIR, '_build'),
        STATIC_ROOT=os.path.join(BASE_DIR, '_build', 'static'),
        STATICFILES_STORAGE='django.contrib.staticfiles.storage.CachedStaticFilesStorage',
    )
    ...
```

With the `STATICFILES_STORAGE` setting in place, our files will get a unique hash associated with them when `DEBUG` is set to `False`. Next we'll need to add our `DEBUG` setting in our `build` management command (located in */sitebuilder/management/commands/ build.py*).

```
    ...
    def handle(self, *args, **options):
        """Request pages and build output."""
        settings.DEBUG = False
    ...
```

Now let's run our management command to see our hashed filenames created in our *build* directory.

```
hostname $ python prototypes.py build
```

When you look inside the *build/static* directory, you should now see your CSS and JavaScript files with unique hashes associated with them. The generated HTML files should also be referencing the hashed names rather than the original name referenced through the {% static %} tag.

While this is a useful technique, there are other packages in the Django community that we can leverage to do even more. In the next section, we'll explore how to use `django-compressor` to compress and minify our CSS and JavaScript files.

Compressing Our Static Files

Another way we can reduce page load is by compressing and minifying our CSS and JavaScript files. `django-compressor` is a common Python package that has been used to assist Django projects in accomplishing this task. It has a few powerful features, such as LESS/Sass compilation.

To start using `django-compressor`, we'll need to install it into our project and then add it to our settings.

```
hostname $ pip install django-compressor
```

Now we'll remove our original caching settings from earlier in this section and add a few required settings to *prototypes.py* that `django-compressor` needs in order for it to work properly.

```
...
settings.configure(
    DEBUG=True,
    SECRET_KEY='b0mqvak1p2sqm6p#+8o8fyxf+ox(le)8&jh_5^sxa!=7!+wxj0',
    ROOT_URLCONF='sitebuilder.urls',
    MIDDLEWARE_CLASSES=(),
    INSTALLED_APPS=(
        'django.contrib.staticfiles',
        'django.contrib.webdesign',
        'sitebuilder',
        'compressor',
    ),
    STATIC_URL='/static/',
    SITE_PAGES_DIRECTORY=os.path.join(BASE_DIR, 'pages'),
    SITE_OUTPUT_DIRECTORY=os.path.join(BASE_DIR, '_build'),
    STATIC_ROOT=os.path.join(BASE_DIR, '_build', 'static'),
    STATICFILES_FINDERS=(
        'django.contrib.staticfiles.finders.FileSystemFinder',
        'django.contrib.staticfiles.finders.AppDirectoriesFinder',
        'compressor.finders.CompressorFinder',
    )
)
...
```

As you can see in the preceding code block, we have added `compressor` to our
`INSTALLED_APPS` listing. We've also added `STATICFILES_FINDER` and the required settings that `django-compressor` needs to work with Django's staticfiles contrib application.

 To see the list of settings to modify `django-compressor` and its default behavior, visit *http://django-compressor.readthedocs.org/en/devel*
op/settings/.

To make our compression happen during our custom build management command,
we'll need to enable compression in *build.py* (located in */sitebuilder/management/*
commands/) and run the `call_command` after collecting the static resources.

```
...
def handle(self, *args, **options):
    """Request pages and build output."""
    settings.DEBUG = False
    settings.COMPRESS_ENABLED = True
    ...
    call_command('collectstatic', interactive=False, clear=True, verbosity=0)
    call_command('compress', interactive=False, force=True)
...
```

Now we can add our `{% compress %}` blocks around our static resources in our *base.html* template (under */sitebuilder/templates*).

```
{% load staticfiles compress %}
<!DOCTYPE html>
...
{% compress css %}
<link rel="stylesheet" href="{% static 'css/bootstrap.min.css' %}">
<link rel="stylesheet" href="{% static 'css/site.css' %}">
{% endcompress %}
...
{% compress js %}
<script src="{% static 'js/jquery.min.js' %}"></script>
<script src="{% static 'js/bootstrap.min.js' %}"></script>
{% endcompress %}
...
```

Let's test our management command with this new configuration using our new settings.

```
hostname $ python prototypes.py build
Found 'compress' tags in:
    /path/to/your/project/sitebuilder/templates/base.html
    /path/to/your/project/sitebuilder/templates/page.html
Compressing... done
Compressed 2 block(s) from 2 template(s).
```

You should now see a *CACHE* folder in your *build* directory that holds your compressed CSS and JavaScript files. The CSS and JavaScript references in the HTML output will also be updated. Not only will the names be updated, but the two stylesheet references should now be one, as should the two `<script>` tags , as you can see in this snippet from *build/index.html*.

```
...
<link rel="stylesheet" href="/static/CACHE/css/00c333162d8e.css" type="text/css" />
...
<script type="text/javascript" src="/static/CACHE/js/a115a2614bdb.js"></script>
...
```

With the default settings for `django-compressor`, these files are just the combination of the two files contained in the block. There are additional settings and configurations available to run these through a minifier such as the YUI compressor.

Instead of using CSS, we could use `django-compressor` to compile the CSS from a preprocessor such as LESS or Sass. Similarly, the JavaScript could instead be built from CoffeeScript. Even though we are using Django in a somewhat unorthodox fashion, the community tools can still help us get the job done.

We can now run the `build` command every time we want to generate any newly compressed and deployable static files. In the next section, we'll generate dynamic content inside of our templates.

Generating Dynamic Content

As you can see so far, rapid prototyping templates in Django have the ability to create a simple website even without a completed backend. The only thing that is missing is the ability to generate dynamic content. One way that other static sites implement that ability is by using a YAML file. Since we don't want to add any unnecessary file infrastructure within our Django application, using this technique is not ideal. Instead, we'll add a few elements to our *views.py* file to be able to utilize dynamic content in our static site.

Updating Our Templates

We have only a few very basic templates in our current static site. Let's add a *pricing.html* template (under */pages*) to add some dynamic content later in this section.

```
{% load webdesign %}
<div class="container">
    <div class="row">
        <div class="col-md-12">
            <h2>Available Pricing Plans</h2>
        </div>
    </div>
    <div class="row">
        <div class="col-md-4">
            <div class="panel panel-success">
                <div class="panel-heading">
                    <h4 class="text-center">Starter Plan - Free</h4>
                </div>
                <ul class="list-group list-group-flush text-center">
                    <li class="list-group-item">Feature #1</li>
                    <li class="list-group-item disabled">Feature #2</li>
                    <li class="list-group-item disabled">Feature #3</li>
                </ul>
                <div class="panel-footer">
                    <a class="btn btn-lg btn-block btn-success" href="#">
                        BUY NOW!
                    </a>
                </div>
            </div>
        </div>
        <div class="col-md-4">
            <div class="panel panel-danger">
                <div class="panel-heading">
                    <h4 class="text-center">Basic Plan - $10 / month</h4>
                </div>
                <ul class="list-group list-group-flush text-center">
                    <li class="list-group-item">Feature #1</li>
                    <li class="list-group-item">Feature #2</li>
                    <li class="list-group-item disabled">Feature #3</li>
                </ul>
```

```
                <div class="panel-footer">
                    <a class="btn btn-lg btn-block btn-danger" href="#">
                        BUY NOW!
                    </a>
                </div>
            </div>
        </div>
        <div class="col-md-4">
            <div class="panel panel-info">
                <div class="panel-heading">
                    <h4 class="text-center">Enterprise Plan - $20 / month</h4>
                </div>
                <ul class="list-group list-group-flush text-center">
                    <li class="list-group-item">Feature #1</li>
                    <li class="list-group-item">Feature #2</li>
                    <li class="list-group-item">Feature #3</li>
                </ul>
                <div class="panel-footer">
                    <a class="btn btn-lg btn-block btn-info" href="#">
                        BUY NOW!
                    </a>
                </div>
            </div>
        </div>
    </div>
    <div class="row">
        <div class="col-md-12">
            <p>{% lorem %}</p>
        </div>
    </div>
</div>
```

Let's also update our *base.html* template (under */sitebuilder/templates*) to include a link to our new page.

```
...
<ul class="nav navbar-nav">
    <li {% if slug == 'index' %}class="active"{% endif %}>
        <a href="/">Home</a>
    </li>
    <li {% if slug == 'pricing' %}class="active"{% endif %}>
        <a href="{% url 'page' 'pricing' %}">Pricing</a>
    </li>
    <li {% if slug == 'contact' %}class="active"{% endif %}>
        <a href="{% url 'page' 'contact' %}">Contact</a>
    </li>
</ul>
...
```

Let's go ahead and do a quick `runserver` command to view what our new pricing page looks like, as shown in Figure 3-6.

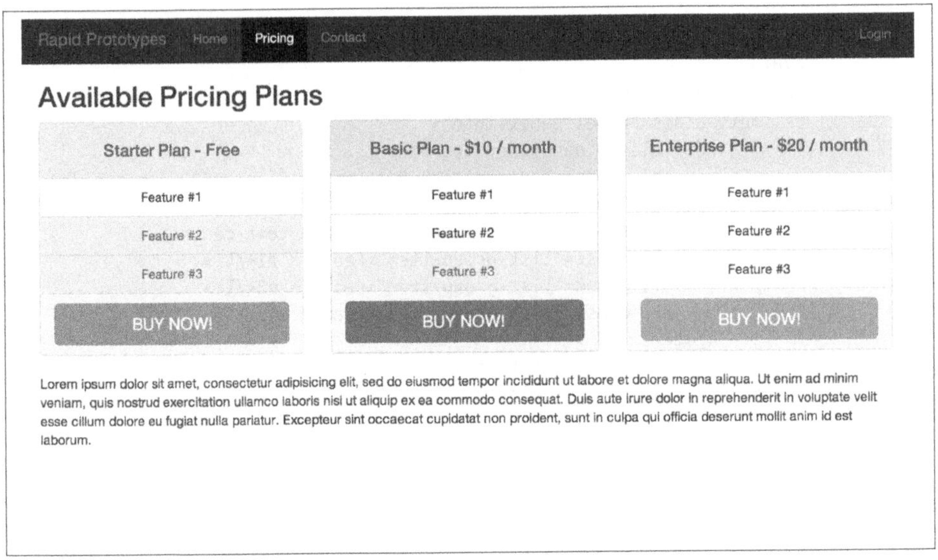

Figure 3-6. Pricing page

While this project seems like it's at a good stopping point, it would be beneficial to the workflow for us to begin thinking about adding dynamic content.

Adding Metadata

To start, we'll refactor our current *views.py* (in the *sitebuilder* folder) to include the ability to read a new {% block %} element that contains our content.

```
import json                                                        ❶
import os
...
from django.template import Template, Context                      ❷
from django.template.loader_tags import BlockNode                  ❸
from django.utils._os import safe_join
...
def get_page_or_404(name):
    """Return page content as a Django template or raise 404 error."""
    try:
        file_path = safe_join(settings.SITE_PAGES_DIRECTORY, name)
    except ValueError:
        raise Http404('Page Not Found')
    else:
        if not os.path.exists(file_path):
            raise Http404('Page Not Found')
```

```
        with open(file_path, 'r') as f:
            page = Template(f.read())

        meta = None
        for i, node in enumerate(list(page.nodelist)):            ➍
            if isinstance(node, BlockNode) and node.name == 'context':
                meta = page.nodelist.pop(i)
                break
        page._meta = meta
        return page


def page(request, slug='index'):
    """Render the requested page if found."""
    file_name = '{}.html'.format(slug)
    page = get_page_or_404(file_name)
    context = {
        'slug': slug,
        'page': page,
    }
    if page._meta is not None:                                    ➎
        meta = page._meta.render(Context())
        extra_context = json.loads(meta)
        context.update(extra_context)
    return render(request, 'page.html', context)
```

➌ ➍ This code loops through the page's raw nodelist and checks for a `BlockNode` with the name `context`. `BlockNode` is a class definition for creating {% block %} elements in Django templates. If the `context` `BlockNode` is found, it defines a metavariable for us that contains that content.

➊ ➋ The metacontext is rendered using Python's `json` module to convert our {% ➎ block context %} into digestible Python.

Now why do we want to load JSON (JavaScript Object Notation) as context into our page? It's important to start thinking about data not only from the database architecture, but also in ways we are easily able to import. For example, if we were to start using a RESTful API to retrieve our data, it would most likely be interpreted from JSON. By starting to think in this way in the rapid prototyping phase, you can more easily make the switch from our simple {% block context %} to dynamically loaded content.

Let's go ahead and test everything out by adding in some context references to our *base.html* template (under */sitebuilder/templates*).

```
{% load staticfiles compress %}
<!DOCTYPE html>
<html lang="en">
<head>
    <meta charset="utf-8">
```

```
<meta http-equiv="X-UA-Compatible" content="IE=edge">
<meta name="viewport" content="width=device-width,initial-scale=1">
<meta name="description"
    content="{{ description|default:'Default prototype description' }}">
<meta name="keywords" content="{{ keywords|default:'prototype' }}">
<title>{% block title %}Rapid Prototypes{% endblock %}</title>
...
```

You can see here that we've added a few new `<meta>` tag references, along with default values. Let's update our new pricing page (*pricing.html* in the *pages* folder) and change those values using our new context blocks.

```
{% load webdesign %}

{% block context %}
{
    "description": "Product Pricing Plans",
    "keywords": "products,pricing,buy me"
}
{% endblock %}

<div class="container">
...
```

Now when you inspect our pricing page's source code, you should see the metadescription and keywords shown in Figure 3-7.

```
<!DOCTYPE html>
▼<html lang="en">
  ▼<head>
      <meta charset="utf-8">
      <meta http-equiv="X-UA-Compatible" content="IE=edge">
      <meta name="viewport" content="width=device-width,initial-scale=1">
      <meta name="description" content="Product Pricing Plans">
      <meta name="keywords" content="products,pricing,buy me">
      <title>Rapid Prototypes - Pricing</title>
      <link rel="stylesheet" href="/static/css/bootstrap.min.css">
      <link rel="stylesheet" href="/static/css/site.css">
    ▶<style>…</style>
    ▶<style id="style-1-cropbar-clipper">…</style>
    </head>
```

Figure 3-7. Pricing page metadata

Now we can easily add and edit dynamic context within our templates. Let's continue by cleaning up our pricing template (*/pages/pricing.html*) even more by using this block to load the pricing plan context.

```
{% load webdesign %}

{% block context %}
{
    "description": "Product Pricing Plans",
```

```
        "keywords": "products,pricing,buy me",
        "plans": [
            {
                "name": "Starter",
                "price": "Free",
                "class": "success",
                "features": [1]
            },
            {
                "name": "Basic",
                "price": "$10 / month",
                "class": "danger",
                "features": [1, 2]
            },
            {
                "name": "Enterprise",
                "price": "$20 / month",
                "class": "info",
                "features": [1, 2, 3]
            }
        ],
        "features": [
            "Feature #1",
            "Feature #2",
            "Feature #3"
        ]
    }
}
{% endblock %}

<div class="container">
    <div class="row">
        <div class="col-md-12">
            <h2>Available Pricing Plans</h2>
        </div>
    </div>
    <div class="row">
        {% for plan in plans %}
            <div class="col-md-4">
                <div class="panel panel-{{ plan.class }}">
                    <div class="panel-heading">
                        <h4 class="text-center">
                            {{ plan.name }} Plan - {{ plan.price }}
                        </h4>
                    </div>
                    <ul class="list-group list-group-flush text-center">
                        {% for feature in features %}
                            <li class="list-group-item
                                {% if forloop.counter not in plan.features %}
                                    disabled
                                {% endif %}">
                                {{ feature }}
                            </li>
```

```
                {% endfor %}
            </ul>
            <div class="panel-footer">
                <a class="btn btn-lg btn-block btn-{{ plan.class }}"
                    href="#">
                    BUY NOW!
                </a>
            </div>
        </div>
    </div>
    {% endfor %}
</div>
<div class="row">
    <div class="col-md-12">
        <p>{% lorem %}</p>
    </div>
</div>
</div>
```

By adding our data via a context block, we can loop through the data just as we would if it were being served externally. The prototyping process has not only considered the layout, but also the way in which we start thinking about how we render our data.

With this exercise you can see that utilizing the Django framework to create a rapid prototyping tool is achievable through a few simple steps and can create a beneficial workflow. The ability for both designers and developers to work in parallel creates an efficient and useful means to create successful end products. While the end goal of this project isn't to create a dynamic website (as Django is commonly used for), we are still able to make use of Django's flexible templating, management command abstractions, and community extensions such as django-compressor.

Some of these same techniques could be applied to single-page web applications where the HTML client is developed using Django, but output and deployed as static HTML. We'll be exploring this more in the upcoming chapter, starting with leveraging Django as a RESTful API server by using the django-rest-framework and its unique browsable interface.

CHAPTER 4

Building a REST API

It's been over a decade since Roy Fielding, an American computer scientist and one of the principal authors of the HTTP specification, introduced REpresentational State Transfer (REST) as an architectural style. Over the years, REST has gained momentum thanks to its popularity for building web services.

By being stateless, and creating unique identifiers for allowing caching, layering, and scalability, REST APIs make use of existing HTTP verbs (GET, POST, PUT, and DELETE) to create, update, and remove new resources. The term REST is often abused to describe any URL that returns JSON instead of HTML. What most users do not realize is that to be a RESTful architecture the web service must satisfy formal constraints. In particular, the application must be separated into a client-server model and the server must remain completely stateless. No client context may be stored on the server and resources should also be uniquely and uniformly identified. The client also should be able to navigate the API and transition state through the use of links and metadata in the resource responses. The client should not assume the existence of resources or actions other than a few fixed entry points, such as the root of the API.

In this chapter, we'll walk through how to utilize the power of RESTful architecture with Django.

Django and REST

Combining Django with REST is a common practice for creating data-rich websites. There are numerous reusable applications in the Django community to help you apply REST's strict principles when building an API. In recent years the two most popular are `django-tastypie` and `django-rest-framework`. Both have support for creating resources from ORM and non-ORM data, pluggable authentication and permissions, and support for a variety of serialization methods, including JSON, XML, YAML, and HTML.

Additional packages with comparisons can be found here: *https://www.djangopackages.com/grids/g/api/*.

In this chapter we will be leveraging `django-rest-framework` to help build our API architecture. One of the best features of this Django reusable application is support for creating self-documenting and web-browsable APIs.

 Filter translation from the query parameters to the ORM isn't built into `django-rest-framework` like it is for `django-tastypie`. However, `django-rest-framework` has pluggable filter backends, and it is easy to integrate with `django-filter` to provide that feature.

We'll start our project by installing all of the necessary dependencies. `Markdown` is used by the browsable API views to translate the docstrings into pages for help when users are viewing the API data.

```
hostname $ pip install djangorestframework Markdown django-filter
```

Now that we have our requirements installed, let's focus on modeling a REST API for a task board.

Scrum Board Data Map

Data modeling is an important first step to any project. Let's take a moment to list all of the points we'll need to consider when creating our models:

- A task board is commonly used in Scrum-style development to manage tasks in the current sprint.
- Tasks are moved from the backlog into the set of tasks to be completed.
- Various states can be used to track the progress along the way, such as "in progress" or "in testing."
- The preceding tasks must be part of a task for it to be in a "completed" state.

One way for visual learners to start understanding how the data interacts is through a visual map, as shown in Figure 4-1.

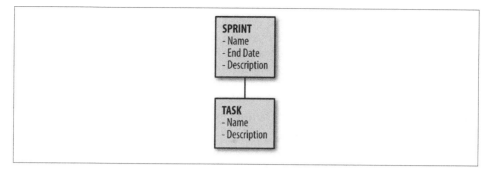

Figure 4-1. Scrum board data map

As you can see, there are multiple steps we'll need to consider when laying out our project. With the aforementioned definitions in place, we can begin laying out the initial project structure.

Initial Project Layout

We'll begin creating our initial project layout by running the base startproject command. While running the command, we'll also be passing in a project named scrum and a single app named board.

```
hostname $ django-admin.py startproject scrum
hostname $ cd scrum
hostname $ python manage.py startapp board
```

Your project's folder structure will be as follows:

```
scrum/
    manage.py
    scrum/
        __init__.py
        settings.py
        urls.py
        wsgi.py
    board/
        migrations/
            __init__.py
        __init__.py
        admin.py
        models.py
        tests.py
        views.py
```

The `startapp` template has evolved in recent Django versions, and the output might be different if you are using a different version of Django. *admin.py* was added to the template in Django 1.6 and the *migrations* folder was added in 1.7.

Let's move on to configuring our *settings.py* file to work with `django-rest-framework` and its inherited settings.

Project Settings

When creating this new Django project, we need to update the default project settings (in *settings.py* in the *scrum* folder) to incorporate `django-rest-framework`, as well as to reduce the defaults from the previous chapters. Also, since the server will not maintain any client state, the `contrib.session` references can be removed. This will break usage of the default Django admin, which means those references can be removed as well.

```
...
INSTALLED_APPS = (                                              ❶
    'django.contrib.auth',
    'django.contrib.contenttypes',
    'django.contrib.staticfiles',
    # Third party apps
    'rest_framework',
    'rest_framework.authtoken',
    # Internal apps
    'board',
)
...
MIDDLEWARE_CLASSES = (                                          ❷
    'django.middleware.common.CommonMiddleware',
    'django.middleware.csrf.CsrfViewMiddleware',
    'django.middleware.clickjacking.XFrameOptionsMiddleware',
)
...
DATABASES = {
    'default': {
        'ENGINE': 'django.db.backends.postgresql_psycopg2',
        'NAME': 'scrum',
    }
}
...
```

❶ These changes remove `django.contrib.admin`, `django.contrib.sessions`, and `django.contrib.messages` from the `INSTALLED_APPS`. The new `INSTALLED_APPS` include `rest_framework` and `rest_framework.authtoken` as well as the *board* app, which will be created in this chapter.

❷ `django.contrib.sessions.middleware.SessionMiddleware,`
`django.contrib.auth.middleware.AuthenticationMiddleware,`
`django.contrib.auth.middleware.SessionAuthenticationMiddleware,` and
`django.contrib.messages.middleware.MessageMiddleware` are part of the
defaults for `startproject` but have been removed from the `MIDDLE`
`WARE_CLASSES` since these applications are no longer installed.

Instead of the default SQLite database, this project will use PostgreSQL. This change
requires installing `psycopg2`, the Python driver for PostgreSQL. We'll need to create the
database as well.

```
hostname $ pip install psycopg2
hostname $ createdb -E UTF-8 scrum
```

 These database settings assume PostgreSQL is listening on the default Unix socket and allows ident or trust authentication for the current user. These settings may need to be adjusted for your server configuration. See Django's documentation (*https://docs.djangopro ject.com/en/1.7/ref/settings/#databases*) for information on these settings.

With the Django admin removed from `INSTALLED_APPS`, the references can also be
removed from the *scrum/urls.py* file.

 If you are an OS X user, we recommend installing Postgres via Homebrew, a package manager specifically for OS X. To learn more and find instructions on how to install Homebrew, see *http://brew.sh/*.

```
from django.conf.urls import include, url

from rest_framework.authtoken.views import obtain_auth_token


urlpatterns = [
    url(r'^api/token/', obtain_auth_token, name='api-token'),
]
```

As you can see, all of the existing patterns have been removed and replaced with a single
URL for `rest_framework.authtoken.views.obtain_auth_token`. This serves as the
view for exchanging a username and password combination for an API token. We'll
also be using the `include` import in the next steps of the project.

No Django Admin?

Some Django developers or users may have a hard time imagining administering a Django project without the Django admin. In this application it has been removed because the API doesn't use or need Django's session management, which is required to use the admin. The browsable API, which will be provided by the `django-rest-framework`, can serve as a simple replacement for the admin.

You may find that you still need to maintain the Django admin due to other applications that rely on it. If that's the case, you can preserve the admin and simply have two sets of settings for the project: one for the API and one for the admin. The admin settings would restore the session and messages apps along with the authentication middleware. You would also need another set of root URLs that include the admin URLs. With these configurations, some servers would serve the admin part of the site and others would serve the API. Given that in a larger application these will likely have very different scaling needs and concerns, this serves as a clean approach to achieving Django admin access.

Models

With the basic structure of the project in place, we can now start on the data modeling portion of our application. At the top level, tasks will be broken up into sprints, which will have an optional name and description, and a unique end date. Add these models to the *board/models.py* file:

```python
from django.db import models
from django.utils.translation import ugettext_lazy as _


class Sprint(models.Model):
    """Development iteration period."""

    name = models.CharField(max_length=100, blank=True, default='')
    description = models.TextField(blank=True, default='')
    end = models.DateField(unique=True)

    def __str__(self):
        return self.name or _('Sprint ending %s') % self.end
```

 While this book is written for Python 3.3+, Django provides a `python_2_unicode_compatible` decorator that could be used to make this model compatible with both Python 2.7 and Python 3. More information on Python 3 porting and compatibility tips can be found in Django's documentation (*https://docs.djangoproject.com/en/1.7/topics/python3/*).

We will also need to build a task model for the list of tasks within a given sprint. Tasks have a name, optional description, association with a sprint (or a backlog in which they're stored), and a user assigned to them, and include a start, end, and due date.

We should also note that tasks will have a handful of states:

- Not Started
- In Progress
- Testing
- Done

Let's add this list of STATUS_CHOICES into our data models (*board/models.py*):

```
from django.conf import settings
from django.db import models
from django.utils.translation import ugettext_lazy as _

...
class Task(models.Model):
    """Unit of work to be done for the sprint."""

    STATUS_TODO = 1
    STATUS_IN_PROGRESS = 2
    STATUS_TESTING = 3
    STATUS_DONE = 4

    STATUS_CHOICES = (
        (STATUS_TODO, _('Not Started')),
        (STATUS_IN_PROGRESS, _('In Progress')),
        (STATUS_TESTING, _('Testing')),
        (STATUS_DONE, _('Done')),
    )

    name = models.CharField(max_length=100)
    description = models.TextField(blank=True, default='')
    sprint = models.ForeignKey(Sprint, blank=True, null=True)
    status = models.SmallIntegerField(choices=STATUS_CHOICES, default=STATUS_TODO)
    order = models.SmallIntegerField(default=0)
    assigned = models.ForeignKey(settings.AUTH_USER_MODEL, null=True, blank=True)
    started = models.DateField(blank=True, null=True)
    due = models.DateField(blank=True, null=True)
    completed = models.DateField(blank=True, null=True)

    def __str__(self):
        return self.name
```

The user reference uses `settings.AUTH_USER_MODEL` to allow support for swapping out the default `User` model. While this project will use the default `User`, the `board` app is designed to be as reusable as possible. More information on customizing and referencing the `User` model can be found at *https://docs.djangoproject.com/en/1.7/topics/auth/customizing/#referencing-the-user-model.*

These are the two models needed for the project, but you can see that there are some clear limitations in this data model. One issue is that this tracks sprints only for a single project and assumes that all system users are involved with the project. The task states are also fixed in the task model, making those states unusable in the sprint model. There is also no support here for customizing the task workflow.

These limitations are likely acceptable if the application will be used for a single project, but obviously would not work if the intention were to build this task board as a software as a service (SaaS) product.

Since we've already written our models, you'll need to run the `makemigrations` and `migrate` commands to have Django update the database properly.

```
hostname $ python manage.py makemigrations board
Migrations for 'board':
  0001_initial.py:
    - Create model Sprint
    - Create model Task
hostname $ python manage.py migrate
Operations to perform:
  Synchronize unmigrated apps: rest_framework, authtoken
  Apply all migrations: contenttypes, auth, board
Synchronizing apps without migrations:
  Creating tables...
    Creating table authtoken_token
  Installing custom SQL...
  Installing indexes...
Running migrations:
  Applying contenttypes.0001_initial... OK
  Applying auth.0001_initial... OK
  Applying board.0001_initial... OK
```

Now we'll create a superuser, with the username of your choosing, using the `createsuperuser` command. For use in future examples, we will assume you create the user with the username *demo* and the password *test*.

```
hostname $ python manage.py createsuperuser
Username (leave blank to use 'username'): demo
Email address: demo@example.com
Password:
Password (again):
Superuser created successfully.
```

Prior to Django 1.7 there was no built-in support for migrated model schemas. Django could create tables only using a single command called syncdb. If you are using a version of Django prior to 1.7, you should run syncdb instead of the aforementioned commands. syncdb will also prompt you to create a superuser and you should create one as outlined in the preceding instructions.

Designing the API

With the models in place, our focus can now shift to the API itself. As far as the URL structure, the API we want to build will look like this:

```
/api/
    /sprints/
        /<id>/
    /tasks/
        /<id>/
    /users/
        /<username>/
```

It's important to consider how clients will navigate this API. Clients will be able to issue a GET request to the API root */api/* to see the sections below it. From there the client will be able to list sprints, tasks, and users, as well as create new ones. As the client dives deeper into viewing a particular sprint, it will be able to see the tasks associated with the sprint. The hypermedia links between the resources enable the client to navigate the API.

We've chosen not to include the version number in the URLs for the API. While it is included in many popular APIs, we feel that the approach for versioning that aligns best with RESTful practices is to use different content types for different API versions. However, if you really want a version number in your API, feel free to add it.

Sprint Endpoints

Building resources tied to Django models with django-rest-framework is easy with ViewSets. To build the ViewSet for the */api/sprints/*, we should describe how the model should be serialized and deserialized by the API. This is handled by serializers and created in *board/serializers.py*.

```python
from rest_framework import serializers

from .models import Sprint


class SprintSerializer(serializers.ModelSerializer):

    class Meta:
```

```
        model = Sprint
        fields = ('id', 'name', 'description', 'end', )
```

In this simple case, all of the fields are exposed via the API.

Let's create the ViewSet in *board/views.py*.

```
from rest_framework import viewsets

from .models import Sprint
from .serializers import SprintSerializer


class SprintViewSet(viewsets.ModelViewSet):
    """API endpoint for listing and creating sprints."""

    queryset = Sprint.objects.order_by('end')
    serializer_class = SprintSerializer
```

As you can see, the `ModelViewSet` provides the scaffolding needed for the create, read, update, delete (CRUD) operations using the corresponding HTTP verbs. The defaults for authentication, permissions, pagination, and filtering are controlled by the `REST_FRAMEWORK` settings dictionary if not set on the view itself.

 The available settings and their defaults are all described in the Django REST framework documentation (*http://www.django-rest-framework.org/api-guide/settings*).

This view will be explicit about its settings. Since the remaining views will need these defaults as well, they will be implemented as a mixin class in *board/views.py*.

```
from rest_framework import authentication, permissions, viewsets

from .models import Sprint
from .serializers import SprintSerializer


class DefaultsMixin(object):                                    ❶
    """Default settings for view authentication, permissions,
    filtering and pagination."""

    authentication_classes = (
        authentication.BasicAuthentication,
        authentication.TokenAuthentication,
    )
    permission_classes = (
        permissions.IsAuthenticated,
    )
    paginate_by = 25
```

```
        paginate_by_param = 'page_size'
        max_paginate_by = 100


    class SprintViewSet(DefaultsMixin, viewsets.ModelViewSet):
        """API endpoint for listing and creating sprints."""

        queryset = Sprint.objects.order_by('end')
        serializer_class = SprintSerializer
```

 DefaultsMixin will be one of the base classes for the API view classes to define these options.

Now let's add in some authentication for the user permissions. The authentication will use either HTTP basic auth or a token-based authentication. Using basic auth will make it easy to use the browsable API via a web browser. This example does not have fine-grained permissions, since we are working on the assumption that all users in the system are a part of the project. The only permission requirement is that the user is authenticated.

Task and User Endpoints

We need the tasks to be exposed on their own endpoint. Similar to our sprint endpoints, we will start with a serializer and then a ViewSet. First we'll create the serializer in *board/serializers.py*.

```
    from rest_framework import serializers

    from .models import Sprint, Task


    ...
    class TaskSerializer(serializers.ModelSerializer):

        class Meta:
            model = Task
            fields = ('id', 'name', 'description', 'sprint', 'status', 'order',
                'assigned', 'started', 'due', 'completed', )
```

While this looks fine at a glance, there are some problems with writing the serializer this way. The status will show the number rather than the text associated with its state. We can easily address this by adding another field status_display to *board/serializers.py* that shows the status text.

```
    from rest_framework import serializers

    from .models import Sprint, Task


    ...
    class TaskSerializer(serializers.ModelSerializer):
```

```
    status_display = serializers.SerializerMethodField('get_status_display')    
```

```

    class Meta:
        model = Task
        fields = ('id', 'name', 'description', 'sprint',
            'status', 'status_display', 'order',
            'assigned', 'started', 'due', 'completed', )

    def get_status_display(self, obj):
        return obj.get_status_display()
```

   `status_display` is a read-only field to be serialized that returns the value of the `get_status_display` method on the serializer.

The second issue with our serializer is that `assigned` is a foreign key to the `User` model. This displays the user's primary key, but our URL structure expects to reference users by their username. We can address this by using the `SlugRelatedField` in *board/serializers.py*.

```
    ...
    class TaskSerializer(serializers.ModelSerializer):

        assigned = serializers.SlugRelatedField(
            slug_field=User.USERNAME_FIELD, required=False)
        status_display = serializers.SerializerMethodField('get_status_display')

        class Meta:
            model = Task
            fields = ('id', 'name', 'description', 'sprint',
                'status', 'status_display', 'order',
                'assigned', 'started', 'due', 'completed', )

        def get_status_display(self, obj):
            return obj.get_status_display()
```

Finally, we need to create a serializer for the `User` model. Now, let's take a moment to remember that the `User` model might be swapped out for another and that the intent of our application is to make it as reusable as possible. We will need to use the `get_user_model` Django utility in *board/serializers.py* to create this switch in a clean way.

```
    from django.contrib.auth import get_user_model

    from rest_framework import serializers

    from .models import Sprint, Task

    User = get_user_model()

    ...
    class UserSerializer(serializers.ModelSerializer):
```

```
    full_name = serializers.CharField(source='get_full_name', read_only=True)

    class Meta:
        model = User
        fields = ('id', User.USERNAME_FIELD, 'full_name', 'is_active', )
```

This serializer assumes that if a custom User model is used, then it extends from
django.contrib.auth.models.CustomUser, which will always have a USER
NAME_FIELD attribute, get_full_name method, and is_active attribute. Also note that
since get_full_name is a method, the field in the serializer is marked as read-only.

With the serializers in place, the ViewSets for the tasks and users can be created in *board/*
views.py.

```
from django.contrib.auth import get_user_model

from rest_framework import authentication, permissions, viewsets

from .models import Sprint, Task
from .serializers import SprintSerializer, TaskSerializer, UserSerializer


User = get_user_model()

...
class TaskViewSet(DefaultsMixin, viewsets.ModelViewSet):
    """API endpoint for listing and creating tasks."""

    queryset = Task.objects.all()
    serializer_class = TaskSerializer


class UserViewSet(DefaultsMixin, viewsets.ReadOnlyModelViewSet):
    """API endpoint for listing users."""

    lookup_field = User.USERNAME_FIELD
    lookup_url_kwarg = User.USERNAME_FIELD
    queryset = User.objects.order_by(User.USERNAME_FIELD)
    serializer_class = UserSerializer
```

Both are very similar to the SprintViewSet, but there is a notable difference in the
UserViewSet in that it extends from ReadOnlyModelViewSet instead. As the name implies, this does not expose the actions to create new users or to edit existing ones through
the API. UserViewSet changes the lookup from using the ID of the user to the username
by setting lookup_field. Note that lookup_url_kwarg has also been changed for con-
sistency.

Connecting to the Router

At this point the `board` app has the basic data model and view logic in place, but it has not been connected to the URL routing system. `django-rest-framework` has its own URL routing extension for handling ViewSets, where each ViewSet is registered with the router for a given URL prefix. This will be added to a new file in *board/urls.py*.

```
from rest_framework.routers import DefaultRouter

from . import views


router = DefaultRouter()
router.register(r'sprints', views.SprintViewSet)
router.register(r'tasks', views.TaskViewSet)
router.register(r'users', views.UserViewSet)
```

Finally, this router needs to be included in the root URL configuration in *scrum/urls.py*.

```
from django.conf.urls import include, url

from rest_framework.authtoken.views import obtain_auth_token

from board.urls import router


urlpatterns = [
    url(r'^api/token/', obtain_auth_token, name='api-token'),
    url(r'^api/', include(router.urls)),
]
```

We have the basic model, view, and URL structure of our Scrum board application, and can now create the remainder of our RESTful application.

Linking Resources

One important constraint of a RESTful application is hypermedia as the engine of application state (HATEOAS). With this constraint, the RESTful client should be able to interact with the application through the hypermedia responses generated by the server; that is, the client should be aware only of few fixed endpoints to the server. From those fixed endpoints, the client should discover the resources available on the server through the use of descriptive resource messages. The client must be able to interpret the server responses and separate the resource data from metadata, such as links to related resources.

How does this translate to our current resources? What useful links could the server provide between these resources? To start, each resource should know its own URL. Sprints should also provide the URL for their related tasks and backlog. Tasks that have been assigned to a user should provide a link to the user resource. Users should provide a way to get all tasks assigned to that user. With these in place, the API client should be able to answer the most common questions while navigating the API.

To give clients a uniform place to look for these links, each resource will have a links section in the response containing the relevant links. The easiest way to start is for the resources to link back to themselves, as shown here in *board/serializers.py*.

```python
from django.contrib.auth import get_user_model

from rest_framework import serializers
from rest_framework.reverse import reverse                       ❶

from .models import Sprint, Task


User = get_user_model()


class SprintSerializer(serializers.ModelSerializer):

    links = serializers.SerializerMethodField('get_links')       ❷

    class Meta:
        model = Sprint
        fields = ('id', 'name', 'description', 'end', 'links', )

    def get_links(self, obj):                                    ❸
        request = self.context['request']
        return {
            'self': reverse('sprint-detail',
                kwargs={'pk': obj.pk},request=request),
        }


class TaskSerializer(serializers.ModelSerializer):

    assigned = serializers.SlugRelatedField(
        slug_field=User.USERNAME_FIELD, required=False)
    status_display = serializers.SerializerMethodField('get_status_display')
    links = serializers.SerializerMethodField('get_links')       ❹

    class Meta:
        model = Task
        fields = ('id', 'name', 'description', 'sprint',
            'status', 'status_display', 'order',
            'assigned', 'started', 'due', 'completed', 'links', )

    def get_status_display(self, obj):
        return obj.get_status_display()

    def get_links(self, obj):                                    ❺
        request = self.context['request']
```

```
                return {
                    'self': reverse('task-detail',
                        kwargs={'pk': obj.pk}, request=request),
                }


    class UserSerializer(serializers.ModelSerializer):

        full_name = serializers.CharField(source='get_full_name', read_only=True)
        links = serializers.SerializerMethodField('get_links')              ❻

        class Meta:
            model = User
            fields = ('id', User.USERNAME_FIELD, 'full_name',
                'is_active', 'links', )

        def get_links(self, obj):                                           ❼
            request = self.context['request']
            username = obj.get_username()
            return {
                'self': reverse('user-detail',
                    kwargs={User.USERNAME_FIELD: username}, request=request),
            }
```

❶   This is a new import for rest_framework.reverse.reverse.

❷ ❹ Each serializer has a new read-only links field for the response body.
❻

❸ ❺ To populate the links value, each serializer has a get_links method to build
❼   the related links.

Each resource now has a new links field that returns the dictionary returned by the
get_links method. For now there is only a single key in the dictionary, called "self",
which links to the details for that resource. get_links doesn't use the standard reverse
from Django, but rather a modification that is built into django-rest-framework. Unlike Django's reverse, this will return the full URI, including the hostname and protocol,
along with the path. For this, reverse needs the current request, which is passed into
the serializer context by default when we're using the standard ViewSets.

A task assigned to a sprint should point back to its sprint. You can also link from a task
to its assigned user by reversing the URL if there is a user assigned, as shown here in
board/serializers.py.

```
    ...
    class TaskSerializer(serializers.ModelSerializer):
    ...
        def get_links(self, obj):
            request = self.context['request']
            links = {
                'self': reverse('task-detail',
```

```
                    kwargs={'pk': obj.pk}, request=request),
                'sprint': None,
                'assigned': None
        }
        if obj.sprint_id:
            links['sprint'] = reverse('sprint-detail',
                kwargs={'pk': obj.sprint_id}, request=request)
        if obj.assigned:
            links['assigned'] = reverse('user-detail',
                kwargs={User.USERNAME_FIELD: obj.assigned}, request=request)
        return links
```

Linking from a sprint or user to the related tasks will require filtering, which will be added in a later section.

Testing Out the API

With the models and views in place for the API, it is time to test the API. We'll explore this first by using the browser, then through the Python shell.

Using the Browsable API

Having a visual tool and creating a browsable API is one of the best features of django-rest-framework. While you may choose to disable it in your production system, it is a very powerful way to explore the API. In particular, using the browsable API helps you think about how a client will navigate through the API by following links given in the responses.

The client should be able to enter the API through a fixed endpoint and explore the API through the resource representations returned by the server. The first step is to get the development server running using runserver:

```
hostname $ python manage.py runserver
Performing system checks...

System check identified no issues (0 silenced).
June 11, 2014 - 00:46:41
Django version 1.7, using settings 'scrum.settings'
Starting development server at http://127.0.0.1:8000/
Quit the server with CONTROL-C.
```

You should now be able to visit *http://127.0.0.1:8000/api/* in your favorite browser to view the API, as seen in Figure 4-2.

Figure 4-2. django-rest-framework API home page

As you can see, this serves as a nice visual tool for viewing our newly made API. It shows the response from issuing a GET to */api/*. It's a simple response that shows the available top-level resources defined by the API. While the API root doesn't require authentication, all of the subresources do; when you click a link, the browser will prompt you for a username and password for HTTP auth. You can use the username and password created previously.

```
HTTP 200 OK
Vary: Accept
Content-Type: application/json
Allow: GET, HEAD, OPTIONS

{
    "sprints": "http://localhost:8000/api/sprints/",
    "tasks": "http://localhost:8000/api/tasks/",
    "users": "http://localhost:8000/api/users/"
}
```

Clicking on the link for sprints will show the resource that lists all the available sprints. At this point none have been created, so the response is empty. However, at the bottom of the page is a form that allows for creating a new sprint. Create a new sprint with the name "Something Sprint," description "Test," and end date of any date in the future. The date should be given in ISO format, YYYY-MM-DD. Clicking the POST button shows the successful response with the 201 status code.

```
HTTP 201 CREATED
Vary: Accept
Content-Type: application/json
Location: http://localhost:8000/api/sprints/1/
Allow: GET, POST, HEAD, OPTIONS

{
    "id": 1,
    "name": "Something Sprint",
    "description": "Test",
    "end": "2020-12-31",
    "links": {
        "self": "http://localhost:8000/api/sprints/1/"
    }
}
```

Refreshing the sprint list shows the sprint in the results, as illustrated in Figure 4-3.

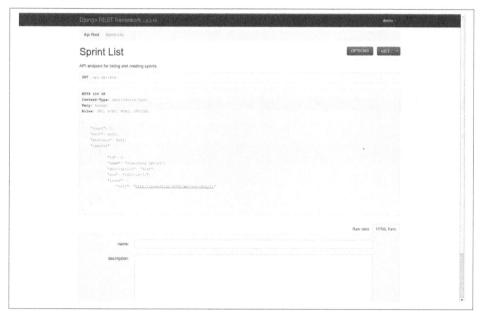

Figure 4-3. Sprints API screenshot

Navigating back to the API root at */api/*, we can now explore the tasks. Similarly to the sprints, clicking the tasks link from the API root shows a listing of all tasks, but there are none yet. Using the form at the bottom, we can create a task. For this task we will use the name "First Task" and the sprint will be the previously created sprint. Again, the API gives a 201 status with the details of the newly created task.

```
HTTP 201 CREATED
Vary: Accept
Content-Type: application/json
Location: http://localhost:8000/api/tasks/1/
Allow: GET, POST, HEAD, OPTIONS

{
    "id": 1,
    "name": "First Task",
    "description": "",
    "sprint": 1,
    "status": 1,
    "status_display": "Not Started"
    "order": 0,
    "assigned": null,
    "started": null,
    "due": null,
    "completed": null,
    "links": {
        "assigned": null,
        "self": "http://localhost:8000/api/tasks/1/",
        "sprint": "http://localhost:8000/api/sprints/1/"
    }
}
```

Refreshing the task list shows the task in the results, as seen in Figure 4-4.

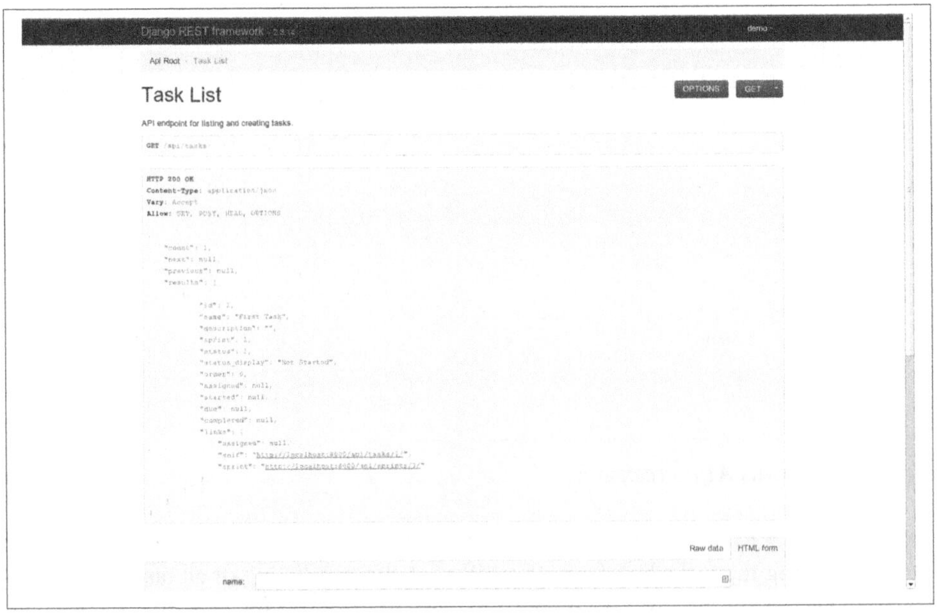

Figure 4-4. Tasks API screenshot

With our basic infrastructure in place for our browsable API, let's add some filtering to further organize the structured page data.

Adding Filtering

As previously mentioned, `django-rest-framework` has support for using various filter backends. We can enable these in all resources by adding them to the `DefaultsMixin` in *board/views.py*.

```
...
from rest_framework import authentication, permissions, viewsets, filters    ❶
...
class DefaultsMixin(object):
    """Default settings for view authentication, permissions,
    filtering and pagination."""

    authentication_classes = (
        authentication.BasicAuthentication,
        authentication.TokenAuthentication,
    )
    permission_classes = (
        permissions.IsAuthenticated,
    )
    paginate_by = 25
    paginate_by_param = 'page_size'
    max_paginate_by = 100
    filter_backends = (                                                        ❷
        filters.DjangoFilterBackend,
        filters.SearchFilter,
        filters.OrderingFilter,
    )
...
```

❶ This adds `filters` to the import list.

❷ DefaultsMixin now defines the list of available `filter_backends`, which will enable these for all of the existing ViewSets.

We configure the `SearchFilter` by adding a `search_fields` attribute to each **ViewSet**. We configure the `OrderingFilter` by adding a list of fields, which can be used for ordering the `ordering_fields`. This snippet from *board/views.py* demonstrates.

```
...
class SprintViewSet(DefaultsMixin, viewsets.ModelViewSet):
    """API endpoint for listing and creating sprints."""

    queryset = Sprint.objects.order_by('end')
    serializer_class = SprintSerializer
    search_fields = ('name', )                                                ❶
    ordering_fields = ('end', 'name', )                                       ❷
```

```
class TaskViewSet(DefaultsMixin, viewsets.ModelViewSet):
    """API endpoint for listing and creating tasks."""

    queryset = Task.objects.all()
    serializer_class = TaskSerializer
    search_fields = ('name', 'description', )                    ❸
    ordering_fields = ('name', 'order', 'started', 'due', 'completed', )   ❹


class UserViewSet(DefaultsMixin, viewsets.ReadOnlyModelViewSet):
    """API endpoint for listing users."""

    lookup_field = User.USERNAME_FIELD
    lookup_url_kwarg = User.USERNAME_FIELD
    queryset = User.objects.order_by(User.USERNAME_FIELD)
    serializer_class = UserSerializer
    search_fields = (User.USERNAME_FIELD, )                      ❺
```

❶ ❸ search_fields are added to all of the views to allow searching on the given list
❺   of fields.

❷ ❹ Sprints and tasks are made orderable in the API using the ordering_fields.
Users will always be ordered by their username in the API response.

Since there is only one task with the name "First Task," searching for "foo" via *http://
localhost:8000/api/tasks/?search=foo* will yield no results, while seaching for "first" with
http://localhost:8000/api/tasks/?search=first will.

To handle additional filtering of the task, we can make use of the
DjangoFilterBackend. This requires defining a filter_class on the TaskViewSet.
The filter_class attribute should be a subclass of django_filters.FilterSet. This
will be added in a new file, *board/forms.py*.

```
import django_filters

from .models import Task


class TaskFilter(django_filters.FilterSet):

    class Meta:
        model = Task
        fields = ('sprint', 'status', 'assigned', )
```

This is the most basic use of django-filter; it builds the filter set based on the model
definition. Each field defined in TaskFilter will translate into a query parameter, which
the client can use to filter the result set. First, this must be associated with the
TaskViewSet in *board/views.py*.

```
...
from .forms import TaskFilter                                                    ❶
from .models import Sprint, Task
from .serializers import SprintSerializer, TaskSerializer, UserSerializer

...
class TaskViewSet(DefaultsMixin, viewsets.ModelViewSet):
    """API endpoint for listing and creating tasks."""

    queryset = Task.objects.all()
    serializer_class = TaskSerializer
    filter_class = TaskFilter                                                    ❷
    search_fields = ('name', 'description', )
    ordering_fields = ('name', 'order', 'started', 'due', 'completed', )
...
```

❶❷ Here the new TaskFilter class is imported and assigned to the
TaskViewSet.filter_class.

With this in place, the client can filter on the sprint, status, or assigned user. However,
the sprint for a task isn't required and this filter won't allow for selecting tasks without
a sprint. In our current data model, a task that isn't currently assigned a sprint would
be considered a backlog task. To handle this, we can add a new field to the TaskFilter
in *board/forms.py*.

```
import django_filters

from .models import Task


class NullFilter(django_filters.BooleanFilter):
    """Filter on a field set as null or not."""

    def filter(self, qs, value):
        if value is not None:
            return qs.filter(**{'%s__isnull' % self.name: value})
        return qs


class TaskFilter(django_filters.FilterSet):

    backlog = NullFilter(name='sprint')

    class Meta:
        model = Task
        fields = ('sprint', 'status', 'assigned', 'backlog', )
```

This will make *http://localhost:8000/api/tasks/?backlog=True* return all tasks that aren't
assigned to a sprint. Another issue with TaskFilter is that the users referenced by
assigned are referenced by the pk, while the rest of the API uses the username as a

unique identifier. We can address this by changing the field used by the underlying ModelChoiceField in *board/forms.py*.

```python
import django_filters

from django.contrib.auth import get_user_model                    ❶

from .models import Task


User = get_user_model()                                           ❷


class NullFilter(django_filters.BooleanFilter):
    """Filter on a field set as null or not."""

    def filter(self, qs, value):
        if value is not None:
            return qs.filter(**{'%s__isnull' % self.name: value})
        return qs


class TaskFilter(django_filters.FilterSet):

    backlog = NullFilter(name='sprint')

    class Meta:
        model = Task
        fields = ('sprint', 'status', 'assigned', 'backlog', )

    def __init__(self, *args, **kwargs):                          ❸
        super().__init__(*args, **kwargs)
        self.filters['assigned'].extra.update(
            {'to_field_name': User.USERNAME_FIELD})
```

❶ ❷ Fetch a reference to the installed User model as we've done in other modules.

❸ Update the assigned filter to use the User.USERNAME_FIELD as the field reference rather than the default pk.

With this change in place, the tasks assigned to the one and only *demo* user can now be retrived using *http://localhost:8000/api/tasks/?assigned=demo* rather than *http://local host:8000/api/tasks/?assigned=1*.

Sprints could also use some more complex filtering. Clients might be interested in sprints that haven't ended yet or will end in some range. For this, we can create a SprintFilter in *board/forms.py*.

```python
...
from .models import Task, Sprint
...
```

```
class SprintFilter(django_filters.FilterSet):

    end_min = django_filters.DateFilter(name='end', lookup_type='gte')
    end_max = django_filters.DateFilter(name='end', lookup_type='lte')

    class Meta:
        model = Sprint
        fields = ('end_min', 'end_max', )
```

And then we relate it to the SprintViewSet in a similar fashion in *board/views.py*.

```
...
from .forms import TaskFilter, SprintFilter
...

class SprintViewSet(DefaultsMixin, viewsets.ModelViewSet):
    """API endpoint for listing and creating sprints."""

    queryset = Sprint.objects.order_by('end')
    serializer_class = SprintSerializer
    filter_class = SprintFilter                              ❶
    search_fields = ('name', )
    ordering_fields = ('end', 'name', )
```

 As with the TaskViewSet, the SprintViewSet now defines a filter_class attribute using the new SprintFilter.

http://localhost:8000/api/sprints/?end_min=2014-07-01 will show all sprints that ended after July 1, 2014, and *http://localhost:8000/api/sprints/?end_max=2014-08-01* will show all sprints that ended before August 1, 2014. These can be combined to limit sprints to a given date range.

Since the views for sprints and tasks support filtering, you can create links to link a sprint to its related tasks and users to their tasks by modifying *board/serializers.py*.

```
...

class SprintSerializer(serializers.ModelSerializer):
...
    def get_links(self, obj):
        request = self.context['request']
        return {
            'self': reverse('sprint-detail',
                kwargs={'pk': obj.pk}, request=request),
            'tasks': reverse('task-list',
                request=request) + '?sprint={}'.format(obj.pk),
        }
...
class UserSerializer(serializers.ModelSerializer):
...
    def get_links(self, obj):
```

```
        request = self.context['request']
        username = obj.get_username()
        return {
            'self': reverse('user-detail',
                kwargs={User.USERNAME_FIELD: username}, request=request),
            'tasks': '{}?assigned={}'.format(
                reverse('task-list', request=request), username)
        }
```

With our filters in place, and to continue the benefits of using this browsable interface, let's build out some validations to secure the state of our data.

Adding Validations

While using the frontend interface can be useful, it doesn't take much exploration through the API to realize that it has some problems. In particular, it allows changes to things that probably should not be changed. It also makes it possible to create a sprint that has already ended. These are all problems within the serializers.

Up until this point, our focus has been on how the model data is serialized into a dictionary to later become JSON, XML, YAML, and so on for the client. No work has been done yet on changing how the client's request of that markup is translated back into creating a model instance. For a typical Django view, this would be handled by a Form or ModelForm. In django-rest-framework, this is handled by the serializer. Not surprisingly, the API is similar to those of Django's forms. In fact, the serializer fields make use of the existing logic in Django's form fields.

One thing the API should prevent is creating sprints that have happened prior to the current date and time. To handle this, the SprintSerializer needs to check the value of the end date submitted by the client. Each serializer field has a validate_<field> hook that is called to perform additional validations on the field. Again, this parallels the clean_<field> in Django's forms. This should be added to SprintSerializer in *board/serializers.py*.

```
from datetime import date                                    ❶

from django.contrib.auth import get_user_model
from django.utils.translation import ugettext_lazy as _      ❷

from rest_framework import serializers
from rest_framework.reverse import reverse

from .models import Sprint, Task


User = get_user_model()


class SprintSerializer(serializers.ModelSerializer):
```

```
links = serializers.SerializerMethodField('get_links')

class Meta:
    model = Sprint
    fields = ('id', 'name', 'description', 'end', 'links', )

def get_links(self, obj):
    request = self.context['request']
    return {
        'self': reverse('sprint-detail',
            kwargs={'pk': obj.pk}, request=request),
        'tasks': reverse('task-list',
            request=request) + '?sprint={}'.format(obj.pk),
    }

def validate_end(self, attrs, source):                              ❸
    end_date = attrs[source]
    new = not self.object
    changed = self.object and self.object.end != end_date
    if (new or changed) and (end_date < date.today()):
        msg = _('End date cannot be in the past.')
        raise serializers.ValidationError(msg)
    return attrs

...
```

❶❷ These are new imports for `datetime` from the standard library and `ugettext_lazy` to make the error messages translatable.

❸ `validate_end` checks that the end date is greater than or equal to the current date for newly created sprints or any sprint that is being updated.

To see this in action, we can attempt to create a historical sprint on *http://localhost:8000/api/sprints/*. You should now get a 400 BAD REQUEST response.

```
HTTP 400 BAD REQUEST
Vary: Accept
Content-Type: application/json
Allow: GET, POST, HEAD, OPTIONS

{
    "end": [
        "End date cannot be in the past."
    ]
}
```

The check for the current object ensures that this validation will apply only to new objects and existing objects where the end date is being changed. That will allow the name of a past sprint to be changed but not its end date.

Similar to this issue, there is also no validation for creating and editing tasks. Tasks can be added to sprints that are already over and can also have the completed date set without being marked as done. Also, the tasks can have their start date set without being started.

Validating conditions that require more than one field is handled in the `validate` method, which parallels the `clean` method for forms, as shown in this snippet from *board/serializers.py*.

```
...
class TaskSerializer(serializers.ModelSerializer):
...
    def validate_sprint(self, attrs, source):                          ❶
        sprint = attrs[source]
        if self.object and self.object.pk:
            if sprint != self.object.sprint:
                if self.object.status == Task.STATUS_DONE:
                    msg = _('Cannot change the sprint of a completed task.')
                    raise serializers.ValidationError(msg)
                if sprint and sprint.end < date.today():
                    msg = _('Cannot assign tasks to past sprints.')
                    raise serializers.ValidationError(msg)
        else:
            if sprint and sprint.end < date.today():
                msg = _('Cannot add tasks to past sprints.')
                raise serializers.ValidationError(msg)
        return attrs

    def validate(self, attrs):                                         ❷
        sprint = attrs.get('sprint')
        status = int(attrs.get('status'))
        started = attrs.get('started')
        completed = attrs.get('completed')
        if not sprint and status != Task.STATUS_TODO:
            msg = _('Backlog tasks must have "Not Started" status.')
            raise serializers.ValidationError(msg)
        if started and status == Task.STATUS_TODO:
            msg = _('Started date cannot be set for not started tasks.')
            raise serializers.ValidationError(msg)
        if completed and status != Task.STATUS_DONE:
            msg = _('Completed date cannot be set for uncompleted tasks.')
            raise serializers.ValidationError(msg)
        return attrs
...
```

❶ `validate_sprint` ensures that the sprint is not changed after the task is completed and that tasks are not assigned to sprints that have already been completed.

❷ `validate` ensures that the combination of fields makes sense for the task.

Since these validations are handled only by the serializers, not the models, they won't be checked if other parts of the project are changing or creating these models. If the Django admin is enabled, sprints in the past can still be added; likewise, if the project adds some import scripts, those could still add historical sprints.

With our validations in place, let's take a look at how we can use a Python client to browse our RESTful API and see how to capture the data with Python.

Using a Python Client

The browsable API is a simple way to explore the API and ensure that the resources link together in a way that makes sense. However, it gives the same experience as how a programmatic client would use the API. To understand how a developer would use the API, we can write a simple client in Python using the popular `requests` library. First, it needs to be installed with `pip`:

```
hostname $ pip install requests
```

In one terminal run the server with `runserver`, and in another start the Python interactive shell. Similar to the browser, we can start by fetching the root of the API at *http://localhost:8000/api/*:

```
hostname $ python
>>> import requests
>>> import pprint
>>> response = requests.get('http://localhost:8000/api/')
>>> response.status_code
200
>>> api = response.json()
>>> pprint.pprint(api)
{'sprints': 'http://localhost:8000/api/sprints/',
 'tasks': 'http://localhost:8000/api/tasks/',
 'users': 'http://localhost:8000/api/users/'}
```

The API root lists the subresources below it for the sprints, tasks, and users. In the current configuration this view does not require any authentication, but the remaining resources do. Continuing in the shell, attempting to access a resource without authentication will return a 401 error:

```
>>> response = requests.get(api['sprints'])
>>> response.status_code
401
```

We can authenticate the client by passing the username and password as the `auth` argument:

```
>>> response = requests.get(api['sprints'], auth=('demo', 'test'))
>>> response.status_code
200
```

Remember, this example assumes that there is a user with the username *demo* and password *test*. You would have set these up during the creation of the database tables in the section "Models" on page 66.

Using this *demo* user, we'll create a new sprint and add some tasks to it. Creating a sprint requires sending a POST request to the sprint's endpoint, giving a name and end date to the sprint.

```
>>> import datetime
>>> today = datetime.date.today()
>>> two_weeks = datetime.timedelta(days=14)
>>> data = {'name': 'Current Sprint', 'end': today + two_weeks}
>>> response = requests.post(api['sprints'], data=data, auth=('demo', 'test'))
>>> response.status_code
201
>>> sprint = response.json()
>>> pprint.pprint(sprint)
{'description': '',
 'end': '2014-08-31',
 'id': 2,
 'links': {'self': 'http://localhost:8000/api/sprints/2/',
           'tasks': 'http://localhost:8000/api/tasks/?sprint=2'},
 'name': 'Current Sprint'}
```

With the sprint created, we can now add tasks associated with it. The URL for the sprint defines a unique reference for it, and that will be passed to the request to create a task.

```
>>> data = {'name': 'Something Task', 'sprint': sprint['id']}
>>> response = requests.post(api['tasks'], data=data, auth=('demo', 'test'))
>>> response.status_code
201
>>> task = response.json()
>>> pprint.pprint(task)
{'assigned': None,
 'completed': None,
 'description': '',
 'due': None,
 'id': 2,
 'links': {'assigned': None,
           'self': 'http://localhost:8000/api/tasks/2/',
           'sprint': 'http://localhost:8000/api/sprints/2/'},
 'name': 'Something Task',
 'order': 0,
 'sprint': 2,
 'started': None,
 'status': 1,
 'status_display': 'Not Started'}
```

We can update the tasks by sending a PUT with the new task data to its URL. Let's update the status and start date and assign the task to the *demo* user.

```
>>> task['assigned'] = 'demo'
>>> task['status'] = 2
>>> task['started'] = today
>>> response = requests.put(task['links']['self'],
        ...data=task, auth=('demo', 'test'))
>>> response.status_code
200
>>> task = response.json()
>>> pprint.pprint(task)
{'assigned': 'demo',
 'completed': None,
 'description': '',
 'due': None,
 'id': 2,
 'links': {'assigned': 'http://localhost:8000/api/users/demo/',
           'self': 'http://localhost:8000/api/tasks/2/',
           'sprint': 'http://localhost:8000/api/sprints/2/'},
 'name': 'Something Task',
 'order': 0,
 'sprint': 2,
 'started': '2014-08-17',
 'status': 2,
 'status_display': 'In Progress'}
```

Notice that throughout this process the URLs were not built by the client but rather were given by the API. Similar to using the browsable API, the client did not need to know how the URLs were constructed. The client explores the API and finds that the resources and logic were about parsing the information out of the server responses and manipulating them. This makes the client much easier to maintain.

Next Steps

With the REST API in place, and some basic understanding of how to use the API with a Python client, we can now move on to using the API with a client written in JavaScript. The next chapter will explore building a single-page web application using Backbone.js on top of this REST API.

CHAPTER 5

Client-Side Django with Backbone.js

Since the 1990s, initially leveraging some type of framework has become a staple of the way in which we create websites, applications, and services. Because frameworks help alleviate the typical overhead associated with the common tasks used to create these things, it is easy to understand their rise in popularity.

When Django was initially released, it was considered a very unique and innovative approach to web development. But let's think about this period of time for web development. Table 5-1 displays the worldwide browser market share in late November 2005.

Table 5-1. Worldwide browser usage statistics for November 2005

Browser	Percentage
Internet Explorer	84.45%
Firefox	11.51%
Safari	1.75%
Opera	0.77%

As you can see, mobile browsers were not even in the scope of these options at the time of Django's release. It wasn't until the first iPhone was announced (2007) that mobile web browsing started to trend upward. Better tools (e.g., jQuery in 2006) also emerged for developing web applications and generating fast and responsive websites.

Since the advent of this new mobile age, creating useful *application programming interfaces* (APIs) is the de facto technique for manipulating data on the client side. Accordingly, various client-side MVC frameworks have been created to help bootstrap the process of handling different kinds of data sets.

Each client-side MVC framework also has varying levels of complexity, learning curves, and feature sets to create its application structure. It's hard sometimes to decide which framework will work best with your application and be most useful for your project.

Figure 5-1 is a simple chart showing the scale of complexity, learning curve, and feature set for some common JavaScript MVC frameworks.

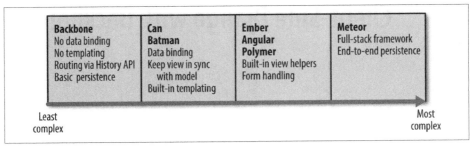

Figure 5-1. JavaScript MVC frameworks chart ordered by level of complexity

Choosing the correct framework is an important decision for you and your team, and you must take a lot of care when considering the aforementioned options. As displayed in Figure 5-1, each of these client-side frameworks has its own level of rich feature sets from which to choose. From Meteor's ability to run on the full stack, to the more simplistic and still feature-rich Angular.js, you can easily get confused about which option is best to use on your Django project.

Because we are focusing more on a leaner and simpler model of development in this book, and less on the rich UI feature sets of other JavaScript frameworks, we've decided to use Backbone for our example project. However, many of the same approaches to code organization and the separation of client and server can be applied to other client-side frameworks.

Brief Overview of Backbone

Backbone was released in late 2010 by Jeremy Ashekenas. It came out of the desire to create a structured and simple approach to a project's JavaScript files throughout the client-side architecture. Backbone is often referred to as the simplest approach to client-side MVC, with only two dependency requirements: Underscore.js and jQuery. Underscore.js (*http://underscorejs.org/*) is a library for adding functional programming utilities—such as `map`, `reduce`, `filter`, `pluck`, and `partial`—that work across browsers. Underscore.js also has a templating engine that compiles into JavaScript functions, which can be evaluated to render HTML or other text from JSON data sources. jQuery (*http://jquery.com/*) is a popular cross-browser DOM manipulation library. It also has utilities for creating the AJAX requests needed by Backbone.

As with any framework, it is important to understand the syntax, layout, and functionality needed to create a project. Let's take a moment to quickly review what models, views, controllers, and routers mean when we are using Backbone.

Models

Models are the main source of information for any Backbone project. They are where the data and the objects that are needed for your application are defined. These map fairly well to Django models.

Collections

Collections are an ordered way to help organize multiple models and the data set within each model. This aspect of an MVC framework helps us manage the different sets and types of application data in an organized way. Collections in Backbone are roughly equivalent to *querysets* in the Django terminology.

Views

Views in Backbone are part of how we create the visual representation of our application, similar to how we use views and templates in Django. They work asynchronously with our models to create dynamic interactions with our application data.

Routers

Routers are a way to create URLs for our application via the History API. Prior to routers, hash fragments were used to create the navigation for a Backbone application. We can connect our routes to actions and events to create a multipage experience in our single-page web application.

With this very basic Backbone foundation of models, collections, views, and routers, you can begin to understand how powerful this very simple framework can be for creating single-page web applications. Now we'll move on to connecting Django and Backbone and working with our REST API from Chapter 4.

 For further reading and tutorials on Backbone, visit the official website (*http://backbonetutorials.com/*).

Setting Up Your Project Files

Recalling our work from Chapter 4, let's have a quick refresher on where we ended up with our Scrum board project. In that chapter, we:

- Created a REST API with `django-rest-framework`
- Started a Django project called `scrum`
- Started a single Django app called `board`
- Added REST API validation with serializers

JavaScript Dependencies

Now we'll need to add a *templates* folder to hold our single-page template. We'll also need to add in a *static* content folder with our client-side dependencies. Here's how our folder structure should be organized:

```
scrum/
board/
  migrations/
  static/
    board/
      css/
      js/
  templates/
  forms.py
  models.py
  serializers.py
  test.py
  urls.py
  views.py
```

Go to the following locations to download Backbone and each of its required dependency files:

- Backbone 1.1.2: *http://cdnjs.cloudflare.com/ajax/libs/backbone.js/1.1.2/backbone.js*
- jQuery 2.1.1: *http://cdnjs.cloudflare.com/ajax/libs/jquery/2.1.1/jquery.js*
- Underscore 1.6.0: *http://cdnjs.cloudflare.com/ajax/libs/underscore.js/1.6.0/underscore.js*

While these files are readily available via the CDN, we'll be downloading them directly into our project to remove the dependency on an Internet connection when we are working locally on the project. We are also using the unminified versions of the libraries since they are easier to debug locally. In a production deployment, you may choose to use the minified versions directly from the CDN or minify them yourself using django-compressor (similar to Chapter 3).

Client-Side Dependency Management

In recent years, there have been numerous competing solutions to solve the problem of client-side dependency management. At this point there is a large amount of fragmentation. Some client-side packages, such as Backbone, are available to install via package managers including npm, bower, volo, jam, and ringojs. If you are interested in a package management solution for your JavaScript and CSS dependencies, bower seems to be emerging as a front-runner, but only time will tell. Perhaps the best client-side package manager is yet to be written.

Once you've downloaded the required files, place them in a new folder called *vendor* inside of our *board/static/board* folder:

```
scrum/
board/
  migrations/
  static/
    board/
      css/
      js/
      vendor/
        backbone.js
        jquery.js
        underscore.js
  forms.py
  models.py
  serializers.py
  test.py
  urls.py
  views.py
```

These files and folders are nested in a *board* folder inside the *static* folder to match the Django convention for namespacing reusable application static resources. Now let's also add a simple *index.html* file to the *board/templates/board* folder to begin the layout portion of the application:

```
scrum/
board/
  migrations/
  static/
    board/
      css/
      js/
      vendor/
  templates/
    board/
      index.html
  forms.py
  models.py
  serializers.py
  test.py
  urls.py
  views.py
```

Similarly, this *index.html* file is inside a *board* folder for the templates to create a namespace for the application templates. Since we are creating a single-page web application, we need only a single template for this project. Typically in Django projects you would create a *templates* folder with multiple templates. Since most of our template code will be written using the `_.template` utility in Underscore.js, however, all of the interactions will happen for our Scrum board project in this single template.

Open up the *index.html* file (in *board/templates/board*) and start laying out the ground-work for our template code dependencies:

```
{% load staticfiles %}
<!DOCTYPE html>
<html class="no-js">
    <head>
        <meta charset="utf-8">
        <meta http-equiv="X-UA-Compatible" content="IE=edge">
        <title>Scrum Board</title>
        <meta name="description" content="">
        <meta name="viewport" content="width=device-width, initial-scale=1">
    </head>
    <body>
        <script src="{% static 'board/vendor/jquery.js' %}"></script>
        <script src="{% static 'board/vendor/underscore.js' %}"></script>
        <script src="{% static 'board/vendor/backbone.js' %}"></script>
    </body>
</html>
```

Load order is important when we're placing our dependencies on the page. Be sure to follow the preceding structure when linking the files for use on your page.

With our folder structure, dependencies, and template now in place, let's start thinking about setting up our actual Backbone application file structure.

Organization of Your Backbone Application Files

Modularity is key in creating a well-structured application. Let's take a moment to relate back to our overview of a simple Backbone template. We learned that we will need—at minimum—models, views, and routers to create a completed application. While we can use a single file to store this code, it doesn't make a lot of sense when we're trying to architect a clean and modular code base.

In your *static/board/js* folder, add in empty files for each portion of the app we'll be writing:

```
scrum/
board/
  migrations/
  static/
    board/
      css/
      js/
        models.js
        router.js
        views.js
```

```
    vendor/
templates/
forms.py
models.py
serializers.py
test.py
urls.py
views.py
```

Let's take a moment to map out the different parts of our new files and what we need from each file. This will be easy for us to reference when we start writing our code.

models.js

Backbone models are where the data of the application is defined and state manipulation occurs. In this file we'll be handling the CSRF (cross-site request forgery) token and the user session management, as well as constructing the data received from our API to display on our page.

views.js

Each Backbone view will consist of the different "pages" we will need for the user to easily navigate around the application. These views will also include form data we'll need for updating sprints and tasks for our Scrum board.

router.js

Simply put, this is where each of the URL paths will be initialized for our application.

Now that we have our project structure in place, we can begin connecting Django to our newly laid-out Backbone application.

Let's add the files we just outlined into our *index.html* page under *board/templates/board*:

```html
{% load staticfiles %}
<!DOCTYPE html>
<html class="no-js">
    <head>
        <meta charset="utf-8">
        <meta http-equiv="X-UA-Compatible" content="IE=edge">
        <title>Scrum Board Project</title>
        <meta name="description" content="">
        <meta name="viewport" content="width=device-width, initial-scale=1">
    </head>
    <body>
        <script src="{% static 'board/vendor/jquery.js' %}"></script>
        <script src="{% static 'board/vendor/underscore.js' %}"></script>
        <script src="{% static 'board/vendor/backbone.js' %}"></script>
        <script src="{% static 'board/js/models.js' %}"></script>
        <script src="{% static 'board/js/views.js' %}"></script>
        <script src="{% static 'board/js/router.js' %}"></script>
    </body>
</html>
```

We'll be placing each file directly below our dependencies, as the code we will be writing relies on them.

Connecting Backbone to Django

A few questions come to mind when we start thinking about the best route to take when connecting Backbone to Django: is there a certain package required to make the connection? What are the specific tasks we need to perform to make a secure connection?

In this section, we'll begin to lay out the context needed to create a clean and reusable infrastructure for our Scrum board application.

In a Django application, the dynamic code that is created on the server side lives inside our template context variables. Since our Django template code is not interchangeable with what our application needs, we'll have to create a digestible way for the data to transfer. We can easily accomplish this by passing our template context variables into something our Backbone application can read: JSON.

Since we've created this file structure to be able to pass variables around our Backbone.js application, let's add some initial null and/or empty values for our models, collections, views, and routers. Open your *index.html* file (under *board/templates/board*) and add the following below the Backbone dependencies:

```
...
<script src="{% static 'board/vendor/backbone.js' %}"></script>
<script id="config" type="text/json">
  {
    "models": {},
    "collections": {},
    "views": {},
    "router": null
  }
</script>
<script src="{% static 'board/js/models.js' %}"></script>
...
```

We'll most likely be reusing these variables throughout various files in our application. Rather than loading them each time, let's create some modularity and build them into an initialization file called *app.js* in our static *js* directory (under *board/static/board*) with the following code:

```
var app = (function ($) {
    var config = $('#config'),
        app = JSON.parse(config.text());

    return app;
})(jQuery);
```

As you can see, we are using a self-invoking function to parse the JSON we created in our template and turn it into variables we can use throughout our application. This returns the parsed configuration values into the `app` global, which can be used by all parts of the application to start configuration and state.

With all of this in place, we are now able to cleanly work in a modular fashion and start building out our client-side infrastructure. Your *index.html* file (located in *board/templates/board*) should now look like this:

```
{% load staticfiles %}
<!DOCTYPE html>
<html class="no-js">
    <head>
        <meta charset="utf-8">
        <meta http-equiv="X-UA-Compatible" content="IE=edge">
        <title>Scrum Board Project</title>
        <meta name="description" content="">
        <meta name="viewport" content="width=device-width, initial-scale=1">
    </head>
    <body>
        <script src="{% static 'board/vendor/jquery.js' %}"></script>
        <script src="{% static 'board/vendor/underscore.js' %}"></script>
        <script src="{% static 'board/vendor/backbone.js' %}"></script>
        <script id="config" type="text/json">
            {
                "models": {},
                "collections": {},
                "views": {},
                "router": null
            }
        </script>
        <script src="{% static 'board/js/app.js' %}"></script>        ❶
        <script src="{% static 'board/js/models.js' %}"></script>
        <script src="{% static 'board/js/views.js' %}"></script>
        <script src="{% static 'board/js/router.js' %}"></script>
    </body>
</html>
```

❶ *app.js* is included after the configuration block but before the project files.

There are now several variables we can utilize throughout our Backbone application. Let's move on to building our routes and see how they interact with our REST API.

Client-Side Backbone Routing

Client-side routes and views are the main components we'll work with when starting to build out the structure in our Backbone application. Yet there is a strong difference between how we normally create routes in Django and how we generate them in our client-side application.

In Django, we create routes for almost every interaction we will encounter. For example, we typically create specific routes for each CRUD (create, read, update, delete) task we need to execute for our application. With Backbone we can take advantage of its stateful nature to encapsulate those tasks within the view and avoid creating unnecessary routes. We'll be showing examples throughout this chapter on how to architect your application to do so.

Let's begin by creating a basic home page view and route for us to begin the foundation of our application's architecture.

Creating a Basic Home Page View

Given that we're building a single-page web application, it is fairly easy to determine where to start: our home page. As mentioned previously in this chapter, our *index.html* file is where most of our template code will live and render to the browser. Let's render the home page template by creating a simple view in our *views.js* file (located in *board/static/board/js*).

```
(function ($, Backbone, _, app) {                    ❶

    var HomepageView = Backbone.View.extend({
```

```
        templateName: '#home-template',                    ❷
        initialize: function () {
            this.template = _.template($(this.templateName).html());    ❸
        },
        render: function () {
            var context = this.getContext(),
                html = this.template(context);
            this.$el.html(html);
        },
        getContext: function () {
            return {};
        }
    });

    app.views.HomepageView = HomepageView;                  ❹

})(jQuery, Backbone, _, app);          ❺
```

❶ ❺ You'll notice a few tools are used in this immediately invoked function expression: jQuery, Backbone, Underscore.js, and App.js. Not only does this make for cleaner code, but it also gives us access to the global variables provided by our *app.js* file. This function expression is based on the JavaScript closure, a function that does not have a return, and helps keep our objects out of the global scope.

❷ We'll need to tell our application what Underscore.js template to render for our home page. We can easily do this by assigning a template name based on the ID selector we'll be using. Keep this in mind in the following section as we start to build our home page template.

❸ We use the Underscore.js `_.template` utility to render our home page template into HTML. This will be handled in a later section.

❹ The HomepageView is added to the `app.views` dictionary so that it can be used in other parts of the application, namely the router.

Now we're ready to set up a router to connect our simple home page view to our page.

Setting Up a Minimal Router

As the previous example shows, it's important to think about how we structure our code to create a sound foundation for future use. In the context of the *router.js* file (in *board/static/board/js*), we'll start out the same way we did with our *view.js* and pass in jQuery, Backbone, underscore.js, and the app configuration global to an anonymous function:

```
(function ($, Backbone, _, app) {
    var AppRouter = Backbone.Router.extend({
        routes: {
            '': 'home'                     ❶
        },
```

```
    \lize: function (options) {
        s.contentElement = '#content';       ❷
         current = null;
          \ne.history.start();

      .e: function () {
        var view = new app.views.HomepageView({el: this.contentElement});
        this.render(view);
    },
    render: function (view) {                 ❸
        if (this.current) {
            this.current.$el = $();
            this.current.remove();
        }
        this.current = view;
        this.current.render();
    }
});

    app.router = AppRouter;                   ❹

})(jQuery, Backbone, _, app);
```

❶ This is where we define our routes for the application. Since we are currently
    concerned only with the home page route, we'll simply add in this singular
    reference.

❷ As laid out in our previous *index.html* structure, this line is where we reference
    the ID selector where our Underscore.js template will load on the page. Calling
    `Backbone.history.start();` will trigger the router to call the first matching
    route for the user.

❸ The `render` function is a helper for the router to track when we are switching
    from one view to another.

❹ Here we attach the router definition to the app configuration to make it available
    in the project scope.

With our home page view and routes in place, we're ready to move forward with building
our first Underscore.js template.

Using __.template from Underscore.js

When developing templates for Django applications, it's best to start out by thinking
about template inheritance and how each template relates to another. When creating a
Backbone application, we typically begin the process by scoping each template into its
own encapsulated portion of code using the powerful library Underscore.js.

Underscore.js is a collection of utilities for creating a functional programming environment with JavaScript. There are over 60 functions that we can utilize to perform the

typical actions we expect when working with a functional programming language. In this section of this chapter, we'll primarily focus on the _.template utility as it relates to writing applications for Backbone.

The _.template utility's main purpose is to create JavaScript templates that compile into functions that can easily be rendered onto the page. As outlined during our views buildout, we'll need to create a home-template in *board/templates/board/index.html* that will serve as a reference to our home page template code.

```
{% load staticfiles %}
<!DOCTYPE html>
<html class="no-js">
    <head>
        <meta charset="utf-8">
        <meta http-equiv="X-UA-Compatible" content="IE=edge">
        <title>Scrum Board</title>
        <meta name="description" content="">
        <meta name="viewport" content="width=device-width, initial-scale=1">
        <script type="text/html" id="home-template">           ❶
            <h1>Welcome to my Scrum Board Project!</h1>
        </script>
    </head>
    <body>

        <div id="content"></div>                                ❷

        <script src="{% static 'board/vendor/jquery.js' %}"></script>
        <script src="{% static 'board/vendor/underscore.js' %}"></script>
        <script src="{% static 'board/vendor/backbone.js' %}"></script>
        <script id="config" type="text/json">
            {
                "models": {},
                "collections": {},
                "views": {},
                "router": null
            }
        </script>
        <script src="{% static 'board/js/app.js' %}"></script>
        <script src="{% static 'board/js/models.js' %}"></script>
        <script src="{% static 'board/js/views.js' %}"></script>
        <script src="{% static 'board/js/router.js' %}"></script>
    </body>
</html>
```

❶ Here we define the home-template. For now it's just static HTML.

❷ A new content div is added to match the selector used by the router.

You'll notice that we've added our home page template into the <head> portion of the page. When thinking about our page load order, we want to make sure that our templates are defined before they might be needed by the view code. Since files load from the top down, we've placed our template code here to ensure they are defined when the view code loads.

The last piece to have the home page to render is to start the router when the page loads. We can do this by initializing the router in *board/static/board/js/app.js*:

```
var app = (function ($) {
    var config = $('#config'),
        app = JSON.parse(config.text());

    $(document).ready(function () {                          ❶
        var router = new app.router();
    });

    return app;
})(jQuery);
```

❶   We also want to make sure that our router does not initialize until the DOM is completely ready for our application to run. While the initial `app.router` will be `null`, it will be added when *router.js* loads. By using jQuery's `$(document).ready` event, we ensure that the `app.router` won't be initialized until after *router.js* has been loaded.

To see this all come together, we need to create a simple Django view *scrum/urls.py* to render *index.html*.

```
from django.conf.urls import include, url
from django.views.generic import TemplateView                ❶

from rest_framework.authtoken.views import obtain_auth_token

from board.urls import router


urlpatterns = [
    url(r'^api/token/', obtain_auth_token, name='api-token'),
    url(r'^api/', include(router.urls)),
    url(r'^$', TemplateView.as_view(template_name='board/index.html')),   ❷
]
```

❶   We are making use of the built-in generic `TemplateView`.

❷   A new pattern is added to route the server root to render the *board/index.html* template.

When you view this in your browser, you should see the output shown in Figure 5-2.

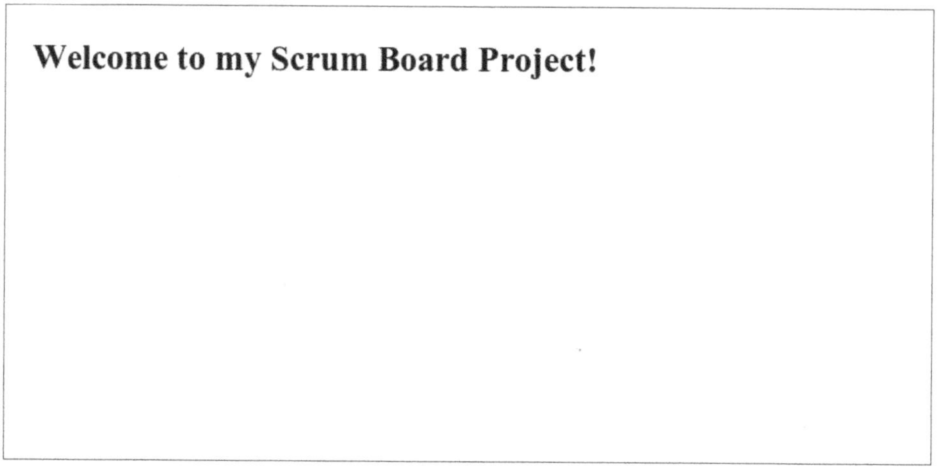

> **Welcome to my Scrum Board Project!**

Figure 5-2. Welcome home page

Congratulations! You have now created your initial setup for our Scrum board application. Let's move on to the next most important component of most web applications: user authentication.

Building User Authentication

In Chapter 4, we enabled the token-based authentication built into `django-rest-framework`. This process expects the user's token to be passed in the `Authorization` header of each request. Recall that this application doesn't make use of Django's default authentication via the session cookie. As we saw when building the Python API client, the client must maintain this state and pass the authentication with every API call. Our next step in that process to create a place for the client to maintain this login state.

Creating a Session Model

As mentioned previously in this chapter, Backbone models are where the data of our application is defined. We generally start our application builds by designing an organized structure of our data.

Sessions are a way in which we can store our API token data to create our user authentication throughout the app. To get started, let's create a basic model for our user session. This will be added in *models.js* in *board/static/board/js/*:

```
(function ($, Backbone, _, app) {

    var Session = Backbone.Model.extend({
        defaults: {                          ❶
            token: null
        },
```

```
            initialize: function (options) {
                this.options = options;
                this.load();
            },
            load: function () {
                var token = localStorage.apiToken;    ❷
                if (token) {
                    this.set('token', token);
                }
            },
            save: function (token) {
                this.set('token', token);
                if (token === null) {        ❸
                    localStorage.removeItem('apiToken');
                } else {
                    localStorage.apiToken = token;
                }
            },
            delete: function () {
                this.save(null);
            },
            authenticated: function () {    ❹
                return this.get('token') !== null;
            }
        });

        app.session = new Session();        ❺

    })(jQuery, Backbone, _, app);
```

There are several things going on in this snippet of code that we'll need in order to process our API token:

❶ This is where we set a default value of null to our token variable. We want to make sure that this variable is already available to us and need to set up its initial value state.

❷ Here is where we are utilizing the initial setup of our token based on the value captured in localStorage.

❸ This code checks whether there is an actual token value. If not, it removes that value and deauthenticates the user.

❹ This method checks for the existence of the token on the current model instance.

❺ This code creates the single instance of the session model needed for the application.

We end by using an immediately invoked function expression to execute only when requested and keeping it out of the global scope. There is one thing missing from the code that we'll need in order to actually work with the HTTP requests being sent. Let's add to *board/static/board/js/models.js* a way to set the request header for our XMLHttpRequest (xhr):

```
(function ($, Backbone, _, app) {

    var Session = Backbone.Model.extend({
        defaults: {
            token: null
        },
        initialize: function (options) {
            this.options = options;
            $.ajaxPrefilter($.proxy(this._setupAuth, this)); ❶
            this.load();
        },
        load: function () {
            var token = localStorage.apiToken;
            if (token) {
                this.set('token', token);
            }
        },
        save: function (token) {
            this.set('token', token);
            if (token === null) {
                localStorage.removeItem('apiToken');
            } else {
                localStorage.apiToken = token;
            }
        },
        delete: function () {
            this.save(null);
        },
        authenticated: function () {
            return this.get('token') !== null;
        },
        _setupAuth: function (settings, originalOptions, xhr) { ❷
            if (this.authenticated()) {
                xhr.setRequestHeader(                                    ❸
                    'Authorization',
                    'Token ' + this.get('token')
                );
            }
        }
    });

    app.session = new Session();

})(jQuery, Backbone, _, app);
```

❷ ❸ An XMLHttpRequest is returned as a JavaScript object that uses a callback method for status changes. It enables us to send an HTTP request to a web server, complete with headers and parameters. In our Session model, you'll notice that we defined a method called _setupAuth. This checks for authentication and if true, passes the token into the requested header parameter in our XMLHttpRequest.

❶ We'll want to actually check to see if the user is authenticated before we initialize our Session model. Here we will use the $.ajaxPrefilter to proxy the token based on the results of our _setupAuth method.

Beyond the authentication token, we'll also need to send the CSRF token with any POST/PUT/DELETE requests. Thankfully, Django has provided snippets to grab the token from the cookie and send it along in the proper header, as shown here in *board/static/board/js/models.js*.

```javascript
(function ($, Backbone, _, app) {

    // CSRF helper functions taken directly from Django docs
    function csrfSafeMethod(method) {                                    ❶
        // these HTTP methods do not require CSRF protection
        return (/^(GET|HEAD|OPTIONS|TRACE)$/i.test(method));
    }

    function getCookie(name) {                                          ❷
        var cookieValue = null;
        if (document.cookie && document.cookie != '') {
            var cookies = document.cookie.split(';');
            for (var i = 0; i < cookies.length; i++) {
                var cookie = $.trim(cookies[i]);
                // Does this cookie string begin with the name we want?
                if (cookie.substring(0, name.length + 1) == (name + '=')) {
                    cookieValue = decodeURIComponent(
                        cookie.substring(name.length + 1));
                    break;
                }
            }
        }
        return cookieValue;
    }

    // Setup jQuery ajax calls to handle CSRF
    $.ajaxPrefilter(function (settings, originalOptions, xhr) {         ❸, ❹
        var csrftoken;
        if (!csrfSafeMethod(settings.type) && !this.crossDomain) {
            // Send the token to same-origin, relative URLs only.
            // Send the token only if the method warrants CSRF protection
            // Using the CSRFToken value acquired earlier
            csrftoken = getCookie('csrftoken');
            xhr.setRequestHeader('X-CSRFToken', csrftoken);
```

```
        }
    });

    var Session = Backbone.Model.extend({
        ...
})(jQuery, Backbone, _, app); ❺
```

❶ ❷ These three helper functions come straight from *https://docs.djangoproject.com/*
❸   *en/1.7/ref/contrib/csrf/#ajax*.

❹   Since this function is self-invoking, these `$.ajaxPrefilter` calls will be made
    when *models.js* is loaded.

❺   Here is where the authentication is handled. If the current session model is
    storing the API token, this token will be added to the `Authorization` request
    header as expected by `django-rest-framework`.

> This assumes that the project is using the default cookie name
> `csrftoken`. If needed, this token could be configured via the config-
> uration parsed by *app.js*.

This will hijack all AJAX requests and add the necessary authentication and CSRF to-
kens. While this is useful, there is still not a way for this code to retrieve the token from
the server. Now that we have a basic structure built out for authenticating our session
data, we need to create a way to authenticate users by creating a login view.

Creating a Login View

Form creation is one of the most important and complicated parts of the web application
development process. It's how users generate content for the Web and therefore should
be well-thought-out.

Our login view will consist of a few different states: initial, error, and success. As we
develop our view, we'll need to structure it in such a way so as not to divert either too
far from or skip these states. Let's start by setting up a basic login view in *board/static/
board/js/views.js*:

```
    ...
    var LoginView = Backbone.View.extend({
        id: 'login',
        templateName: '#login-template',
        initialize: function () {
            this.template = _.template($(this.templateName).html());
        },
        render: function () {
            var context = this.getContext(),
                html = this.template(context);
```

```
            this.$el.html(html);
        },
        getContext: function () {
            return {};
        }
    });
    ...
```

You should define this view within the self-invoking function defined in *views.js*. Going forward, you should assume that any partial code blocks shown for a JavaScript file should be written inside the self-invoking function unless otherwise noted.

As you can see, this view is very similar to the home page view that we previously built. Since we know that we will need to create more views with this same pattern to complete our application, let's leverage Backbone's extendability and create a generic view template in *board/static/board/js/views.js*, upon which we will model all of our views.

```
    ...
    var TemplateView = Backbone.View.extend({
        templateName: '',
        initialize: function () {
            this.template = _.template($(this.templateName).html());
        },
        render: function () {
            var context = this.getContext(),
                html = this.template(context);
            this.$el.html(html);
        },
        getContext: function () {
            return {};
        }
    });
    ...
```

Now we can utilize this template to create each view and apply a DRY ("don't repeat yourself") approach to our code. Our view (*board/static/board/js/views.js*) should now look something like this:

```
    ...
    var TemplateView = Backbone.View.extend({
        templateName: '',
        initialize: function () {
            this.template = _.template($(this.templateName).html());
        },
        render: function () {
            var context = this.getContext(),
                html = this.template(context);
            this.$el.html(html);
        },
        getContext: function () {
            return {};
        }
```

```
  });

  var HomepageView = TemplateView.extend({          ❶
      templateName: '#home-template'
  });

  var LoginView = TemplateView.extend({             ❷
      id: 'login',
      templateName: '#login-template'
  });

  app.views.HomepageView = HomepageView;            ❸
  app.views.LoginView = LoginView;
  ...
```

❶❷ Both the `HomepageView` and `LoginView` now extend from this base `TemplateView`, which cleans up the repeated code.

❸ `HomepageView` and `LoginView` are added to the `app.views` dictionary. `TemplateView` is an implementation detail that isn't needed outside of *views.js* and so it remains hidden.

By creating this generic template, you can easily see how useful it is for developing Backbone applications. However, the `LoginView` must do much more than just render a template. It needs to render the login form, handle the submission, and check on whether it might be successful.

 The Backbone community has a number of extensions meant to reduce some of the same boilerplate code as we are doing here with `TemplateView`. These extensions include MarionetteJS (a.k.a. Backbone.Marionette), Thorax, Chaplin, and Vertebrae. You may consider using one of these extensions if you aren't interested in writing some of these base classes yourself.

Let's start by adding the `login-template` to our *index.html* file (located in *board/templates/board*).

```
  ...
  <script type="text/html" id="login-template">
    <form action="" method="post">
        <label for="id_username">Username</label>
        <input id="id_username" type="text" name="username"
            maxlength="30" required />
        <label for="id_password">Password</label>
        <input id="id_password" type="password"
            name="password" required />
        <button type="submit">Login</button>
    </form>
  </script>
```

```
</head>
...
```

The form contains two inputs, `username` and `password`, that match what is required by the `obtain_auth_token` view. With the template now defined, the view needs to handle the form submission. Backbone view can bind events for the elements it controls using the `events` mapping interface, as shown here in *board/static/board/js/views.js*.

```
...
var LoginView = TemplateView.extend({
    id: 'login',
    templateName: '#login-template',
    events: {                                                    ❶
        'submit form': 'submit'
    },
    submit: function (event) {                                   ❷
        var data = {};
        event.preventDefault();
        this.form = $(event.currentTarget);
        data = {
            username: $(':input[name="username"]', this.form).val(),
            password: $(':input[name="password"]', this.form).val()
        };
        // TODO: Submit the login form
    }
});
...
```

❶ This event property listens for all `submit` events on any form element inside the `LoginView`'s element. When an event is triggered, it will execute the `submit` callback.

❷ The `submit` callback prevents the submission of the form so that the view can submit it and handle the results.

 You can read more about Backbone's view event binding in the official docs (*http://backbonejs.org/#View-delegateEvents*).

During the execution of the `submit` method, the username and password are fetched from the form values. The view doesn't yet know which URL to submit this information to. We know from the project URLs defined in Chapter 4 that this information should be `/api/token/`. We can make use of the app configuration parsed by our *app.js* file to configure this information on the client, as shown here in *board/templates/board/index.html*.

```
...
<script id="config" type="text/json">
    {
        "models": {},
        "collections": {},
        "views": {},
        "router": null,
        "apiRoot": "{% url 'api-root' %}",                         ❶
        "apiLogin": "{% url 'api-token' %}"
    }
</script>
...
```

❶   This adds two new configurations: one for the root of the API, and one for the
     API login URL.

By using the url template tag, we are able to keep the client in line with the URL patterns
defined on our Django backend. This helps avoid any issues with changes that might
happen to either the api-root or api-token in the future.

With this information, the client can now submit to the correct login view in connection
with our API, as shown here in *board/static/board/js/views.js*.

```
...
var LoginView = TemplateView.extend({
    id: 'login',
    templateName: '#login-template',
    events: {
        'submit form': 'submit'
    },
    submit: function (event) {
        var data = {};
        event.preventDefault();
        this.form = $(event.currentTarget);
        data = {
            username: $(':input[name="username"]', this.form).val(),
            password: $(':input[name="password"]', this.form).val()
        };
        $.post(app.apiLogin, data)                                 ❶
            .success($.proxy(this.loginSuccess, this))
            .fail($.proxy(this.loginFailure, this));
    },
    loginSuccess: function (data) {                                ❷
        app.session.save(data.token);
        this.trigger('login', data.token);
    },
    loginFailure: function (xhr, status, error) {                 ❸
        var errors = xhr.responseJSON;
        this.showErrors(errors);
    },
    showErrors: function (errors) {
```

```
              // TODO: Show the errors from the response
        }
    });
    ...
```

❶   By using the new `app.apiLogin` configuration, the username and password
    information is submitted to the backend.

❷   When the login is successful, the token is saved using the previously defined
    `app.session` and a `login` event is triggered.

❸   On failure, the errors need to be displayed to the user.

You'll notice that we've also now included errors into our `LoginView`. The errors will be
returned as JSON and have keys matching the field names with a list of those errors, or
errors that are not associated with a particular field.

```
{"username": ["This field is required."], "password": ["This field is required."]}

{"non_field_errors": ["Unable to login with provided credentials."]}
```

Now we'll need to add a way to make the errors appear somewhere on the form. Let's
update our `showErrors` custom method in *board/static/board/js/views.js* to map to the
field and nonfield errors at the top of the form.

```
    ...
    var LoginView = TemplateView.extend({
        id: 'login',
        templateName: '#login-template',
        errorTemplate: _.template('<span class="error"><%- msg %></span>'),      ❶
        events: {
            'submit form': 'submit'
        },
        submit: function (event) {
            var data = {};
            event.preventDefault();
            this.form = $(event.currentTarget);
            this.clearErrors();                                                   ❷
            data = {
                username: $(':input[name="username"]', this.form).val(),
                password: $(':input[name="password"]', this.form).val()
            };
            $.post(app.apiLogin, data)
                .success($.proxy(this.loginSuccess, this))
                .fail($.proxy(this.loginFailure, this));
        },
        loginSuccess: function (data) {
            app.session.save(data.token);
            this.trigger('login', data.token);
        },
        loginFailure: function (xhr, status, error) {
            var errors = xhr.responseJSON;
```

```
            this.showErrors(errors);
        },
        showErrors: function (errors) {
            _.map(errors, function (fieldErrors, name) {                        ❸
                var field = $(':input[name=' + name + ']', this.form),
                    label = $('label[for=' + field.attr('id') + ']', this.form);
                if (label.length === 0) {
                    label = $('label', this.form).first();
                }
                function appendError(msg) {
                    label.before(this.errorTemplate({msg: msg}));             ❹
                }
                _.map(fieldErrors, appendError, this);                        ❺
            }, this);
        },
        clearErrors: function () {                                            ❻
            $('.error', this.form).remove();
        }
    });
    ...
```

❸ ❺ This loops over all the fields and errors in the response and adds each error to the DOM just before the fields label. If no matching field is found, the error is added before the first label.

❶ ❹ Each error message is created from a new error template that makes use of a new inline Underscore.js template we created at the top of the script.

❷ ❻ This method removes any existing errors from the form on each submission.

Our LoginView now contains all the necessary logic for handling the login form's rendering and submission. Now we need to connect it to a router to display properly. Before doing that, let's see if we can make this form handling more generic so that it can be used later by other views.

Generic Form View

Since we know that we will most likely have more than one form in our application, let's utilize this pattern to create a cleaner code base with a generic FormView to extend upon. We know that we'll need a way for our form to include submission and error handling, so let's begin by adding those components in *board/static/board/js/views.js*.

```
...
var TemplateView = Backbone.View.extend({
    templateName: '',
    initialize: function () {
        this.template = _.template($(this.templateName).html());
    },
    render: function () {
        var context = this.getContext(),
```

```
            html = this.template(context);
        this.$el.html(html);
    },
    getContext: function () {
        return {};
    }
});

var FormView = TemplateView.extend({
    events: {                                                              ❶
        'submit form': 'submit'
    },
    errorTemplate: _.template('<span class="error"><%- msg %></span>'),    ❷
    clearErrors: function () {                                             ❸
        $('.error', this.form).remove();
    },
    showErrors: function (errors) {                                        ❹
        _.map(errors, function (fieldErrors, name) {
            var field = $(':input[name=' + name + ']', this.form),
                label = $('label[for=' + field.attr('id') + ']', this.form);
            if (label.length === 0) {
                label = $('label', this.form).first();
            }
            function appendError(msg) {
                label.before(this.errorTemplate({msg: msg}));
            }
            _.map(fieldErrors, appendError, this);
        }, this);
    },
    serializeForm: function (form) {                                       ❺
        return _.object(_.map(form.serializeArray(), function (item) {
            // Convert object to tuple of (name, value)
            return [item.name, item.value];
        }));
    },
    submit: function (event) {                                             ❻
        event.preventDefault();
        this.form = $(event.currentTarget);
        this.clearErrors();
    },
    failure: function (xhr, status, error) {                               ❼
        var errors = xhr.responseJSON;
        this.showErrors(errors);
    },
    done: function (event) {                                               ❽
        if (event) {
            event.preventDefault();
        }
        this.trigger('done');
        this.remove();
    }
```

```
    });
    ...
```

❶ ❷ events, errorTemplate, clearErrors, showErrors, and failure come directly
❸ ❹ from our original LoginView implementation.
❼

❺ serializeForm is a more generic serialization of the form field values rather
than the explicit version that was present in the LoginView.

❻ submit sets up the start of the form submission by preventing the default
submission and clearing the errors. Each view that extends this will need to
further define this callback.

❽ done is also new, and is a more generic version of triggering the login event. It
also handles removing the form from the DOM, which is what we will want in
most cases.

Like the TemplateView we previously created, this view won't need to be added to the
app.views mapping. Let's see in *board/static/board/js/views.js* how this new FormView
should be applied to our original LoginView.

```
    ...
    var LoginView = FormView.extend({                              ❶
        id: 'login',
        templateName: '#login-template',
        submit: function (event) {
            var data = {};
            FormView.prototype.submit.apply(this, arguments);     ❷
            data = this.serializeForm(this.form);                 ❸
            $.post(app.apiLogin, data)                            ❹
                .success($.proxy(this.loginSuccess, this))
                .fail($.proxy(this.failure, this));
        },
        loginSuccess: function (data) {                           ❺
            app.session.save(data.token);
            this.done();
        }
    });
    ...
```

❶ The LoginView now extends from FormView rather than the TemplateView.

❷ The submit callback calls the original FormView submit to prevent the
submission and clear any errors.

❸ Instead of the username and password fields being retrieved manually, the form
data is serialized with the serializeForm helper.

❹ ❺ The loginSuccess callback now uses the done helper after saving the token. The
default failure callback is used and doesn't have to be redefined here.

JavaScript doesn't have a super call like Python. `FormView.prototype.submit.apply` is the effective equivalent to call the parent method.

As you can see, this work helps simplify our implementation of `LoginView`. At the same time, it creates a base `FormView` for later usage. Now let's move into routes and how we connect our views to them.

Authenticating Routes

As defined earlier in this chapter, Backbone routes are a way to create URLs for our application via the History API. Other than the API root and the login, the API requires some sort of authentication for users to interact with our application. The client won't be able to do anything without the authentication token. We'll need to create a way to display the login form if the token is not available, and be able to fetch it. On the server, we would handle this by redirecting the user to a login URL and redirecting back after the login was established. On the client, the `LoginView` doesn't need a route of its own. We can handle this by hijacking the application routing through our *router.js* file (located in *board/static/board/js*).

```
...
var AppRouter = Backbone.Router.extend({
    routes: {
        '': 'home'
    },
    initialize: function (options) {
        this.contentElement = '#content';
        this.current = null;
        Backbone.history.start();
    },
    home: function () {
        var view = new app.views.HomepageView({el: this.contentElement});
        this.render(view);
    },
    route: function (route, name, callback) {                           ❶
        // Override default route to enforce login on every page
        var login;
        callback = callback || this[name];
        callback = _.wrap(callback, function (original) {               ❷
            var args = _.without(arguments, original);
            if (app.session.authenticated()) {
                original.apply(this, args);                            ❸
            } else {
                // Show the login screen before calling the view
                $(this.contentElement).hide();
                // Bind original callback once the login is successful  ❹
```

```
                        login = new app.views.LoginView();
                        $(this.contentElement).after(login.el);
                        login.on('done', function () {
                            $(this.contentElement).show();
                            original.apply(this, args);
                        }, this);
                        // Render the login form
                        login.render();
                    }
                });
                return Backbone.Router.prototype.route.apply(this, [route, name, callback]);   ❺
            },
        render: function (view) {
            if (this.current) {
                this.current.undelegateEvents();
                this.current.$el = $();
                this.current.remove();
            }
            this.current = view;
            this.current.render();
        }
    });
    ...
```

❶ This overrides the default route method for the router. It is passed as a hash route and either the name of the callback method or an explicit callback function.

❷ The original callback function will be wrapped to first check the authentication state before calling.

❸ If the user is authenticated, then the original callback is simply called.

❹ If the user is not authenticated, then the current page content is hidden and the login view is rendered instead. When the login view triggers a done event, the original callback is allowed to proceed.

❺ The original route is called using the new wrapped callback.

Since users can log in, it would be helpful for them to be able to log out as well. We can handle this with a small view to render a header for the page and create an easy way for users to log out via any portion of the application.

Creating a Header View

Unlike Django views, Backbone views do not need to control the entire page rendering and the page can be handled by multiple views. While the HomepageView will render the main body content, a new HeaderView will be used to render a header that displays at the top of all views. Let's start by adding this template to our *index.html* file (in *board/ templates/board*).

```
...
<script type="text/html" id="header-template">
    <span class="title">Scrum Board Example</span>
    <% if (authenticated ) { %>
        <nav>
            <a href="/" class="button">Your Sprints</a>
            <a href="#" class="logout button">Logout</a>
        </nav>
    <% } %>
</script>
</head>
...
```

As with the other templates, this one will be added to the `<head>` element. This is the first template that makes use of Underscore's template logic. Within `<% .. %>` (notation sometimes referred to as *bee stings*), Underscore can execute JavaScript—in this case, an `if` statement. The value of `authenticated` will be determined by the data used to render the template.

We now should create a view in *board/static/board/js/views.js* to be associated with this template and include the authentication requirements to add our logout interaction.

```
...
var HeaderView = TemplateView.extend({                              ❶
    tagName: 'header',                                              ❷
    templateName: '#header-template',
    events: {
        'click a.logout': 'logout'                                 ❸
    },
    getContext: function () {                                       ❹
        return {authenticated: app.session.authenticated()};
    },
    logout: function (event) {                                      ❺
        event.preventDefault();
        app.session.delete();
        window.location = '/';
    }
});

app.views.HomepageView = HomepageView;
app.views.LoginView = LoginView;
app.views.HeaderView = HeaderView;                                 ❻
```

❶ The `HeaderView` extends from `TemplateView` to keep the logic similar to other views.

❷ Unlike previous views, the `tagName` is defined. This means the template renders into a `<header>` element.

❸ ❺ The nav in the header will have two links when the user is authenticated. One will go back to the home page, and the other will log out. The logout logic is handled in the `logout` callback in the view.

❹ The `authenticated` value is passed to the template context based on the current session state. It won't automatically be updated if this state changes. The view will have to be rendered again.

❻ Finally, the view is added to the `app.views` mapping so that it can be used by the router.

As with the `LoginView`, the `HeaderView` isn't associated with a particular route. It's always present. It needs to change only when the login state changes. This can all be handled within the router itself (i.e., in *board/static/board/js/router.js*).

```
...
var AppRouter = Backbone.Router.extend({
    routes: {
        '': 'home'
    },
    initialize: function (options) {
        this.contentElement = '#content';
        this.current = null;
        this.header = new app.views.HeaderView();          ❶
        $('body').prepend(this.header.el);
        this.header.render();
        Backbone.history.start();
    },
    home: function () {
        var view = new app.views.HomepageView({el: this.contentElement});
        this.render(view);
    },
    route: function (route, name, callback) {
        // Override default route to enforce login on every page
        var login;
        callback = callback || this[name];
        callback = _.wrap(callback, function (original) {
            var args = _.without(arguments, original);
            if (app.session.authenticated()) {
                original.apply(this, args);
            } else {
                // Show the login screen before calling the view
                $(this.contentElement).hide();
                // Bind original callback once the login is successful
                login = new app.views.LoginView();
                $(this.contentElement).after(login.el);
                login.on('done', function () {
                    this.header.render();                    ❷
                    $(this.contentElement).show();
                    original.apply(this, args);
                }, this);
```

```
                        // Render the login form
                        login.render();
                }
            });
            return Backbone.Router.prototype.route.apply(this, [route, name, callback]);
        },
        render: function (view) {
            if (this.current) {
                this.current.$el = $();
                this.current.remove();
            }
            this.current = view;
            this.current.render();
        }
    });
    ...
```

❶   The header view is initialized when the router is created and its element is added
      to the start of the <body>.

❷   When the login is finished, the header is rendered again to reflect the new state.

Separating the hijacking of all of the routes and enforcing the logic and the header from
the main content help ensure that each route doesn't have to deal with the login state
individually, both within the view and its templates.

Why No Login Route?

You might be asking "why don't you simply create a login route and redirect the user?" This is how you would typically handle this in a server-side MVC application, but that's because the server is stateless. On the client side it simply isn't needed. Building rich-client applications is more on a par with building desktop or native mobile applications than server-side web applications. Client-side routes aren't needed for actions such as login, logout, or deleting. Routes are another way for the client to manage state. They make the client-side application linkable and able to be bookmarked. You'll find that adding routes for actions or doing the equivalent of "redirects" on the client side will break the use of the browser's back button or add unnecessary complication to handle the user going back to a view when it wasn't expected.

With the previous approach, these problems are avoided. The login view will never be called if the user is not authenticated, and likewise the HomepageView and the views we will build later will never be called unless the user is authenticated. This encapsulates all of the authentication requirements in one place and doesn't create an unnecessary #login entry in the user's browser history.

Before moving on to more interactions with the API, let's add some basic styles to the site header and login form. To have a clean starting point for adding styles, we'll begin by including a reset stylesheet. This can be downloaded from *http://necolas.github.io/ normalize.css/latest/normalize.css* and should be saved to the *vendor* static directory. We will also be creating our site CSS in *board/static/board/css/board.css*.

```
@import url(http://fonts.googleapis.com/css?family=Lato:300,400,700,900);

/* Generic
==================== */
body {
    -moz-box-sizing: border-box;
         box-sizing: border-box;
    font-family: 'Lato', Helvetica, sans-serif;
}

a { text-decoration: none; }

button, a.button {
    font-size: 13px;
    padding: 5px 8px;
    border: 2px solid #222;
    background-color: #FFF;
    color: #222;
    transition: background 200ms ease-out;
}
```

```css
button:hover, a.button:hover {
    background-color: #222;
    color: #FFF;
}

input, textarea {
    background: white;
    font-family: inherit;
    border: 1px solid #cccccc;
    box-shadow: inset 0 1px 2px rgba(0,0,0,0.1);
    display: block;
    font-size: 18px;
    margin: 0 0 16px 0;
    padding: 8px
}

#content {
    padding-left: 25px;
    padding-right: 25px;
}

.hide {
    display: none;
}

.error {
    color: #cd0000;
    margin: 8px 0;
    display: block;
}

/* Header
==================== */

header {
    height: 45px;
    line-height: 45px;
    border-bottom: 1px solid #CCC;
}

header .title {
    font-weight: 900;
    padding-left: 25px;
}

header nav {
    display: inline-block;
    float: right;
    padding-right: 25px;
}

header nav a {
```

```css
        margin-left: 8px;
    }

    header nav a:hover {
        background: #222;
        color: #FFF;
    }

    /* Login
    ==================== */

    #login {
        width: 100%;
    }

    #login form {
        width: 300px;
        margin: 0 auto;
        padding: 25px;
    }

    #login form input {
        margin-bottom: 15px;
    }

    #login form label, #login form input {
        display: block;
    }
```

Finally, these need to be added to *board/templates/board/index.html.*

```html
{% load staticfiles %}
<!DOCTYPE html>
<html class="no-js">
    <head>
        <meta charset="utf-8">
        <meta http-equiv="X-UA-Compatible" content="IE=edge">
        <title>Scrum Board</title>
        <meta name="description" content="">
        <meta name="viewport" content="width=device-width, initial-scale=1">
        <link rel="stylesheet" href="{% static 'board/vendor/normalize.css' %}">   ❶
        <link rel="stylesheet" href="{% static 'board/css/board.css' %}">           ❷
        <script type="text/html" id="home-template">
            <h1>Welcome to my Scrum Board Project!</h1>
        </script>
        <script type="text/html" id="login-template">
          <form action="" method="post">
            <label for="id_username">Username</label>
            <input id="id_username" type="text" name="username"
                maxlength="30" required />
            <label for="id_password">Password</label>
            <input id="id_password" type="password"
                name="password" required />
```

```
                <button type="submit">Login</button>
            </form>
        </script>
        <script type="text/html" id="header-template">
            <span class="title">Scrum Board Example</span>
            <% if (authenticated ) { %>
                <nav>
                    <a href="/">Sprints</a>
                    <a class="logout" href="#">Logout</a>
                </nav>
            <% } %>
        </script>
    </head>
    <body>

        <div id="content"></div>

        <script src="{% static 'board/vendor/jquery.js' %}"></script>
        <script src="{% static 'board/vendor/underscore.js' %}"></script>
        <script src="{% static 'board/vendor/backbone.js' %}"></script>
        <script id="config" type="text/json">
            {
                "models": {},
                "collections": {},
                "views": {},
                "router": null,
                "apiRoot": "{% url 'api-root' %}",
                "apiLogin": "{% url 'api-token' %}"
            }
        </script>
        <script src="{% static 'board/js/app.js' %}"></script>
        <script src="{% static 'board/js/models.js' %}"></script>
        <script src="{% static 'board/js/views.js' %}"></script>
        <script src="{% static 'board/js/router.js' %}"></script>
    </body>
</html>
```

❶ *normalize.css* provides a consistent cross-browser base for applying styles.

❷ *board.css* is where we are adding our project styles.

If you render the page without authentication, it should look like Figure 5-3.

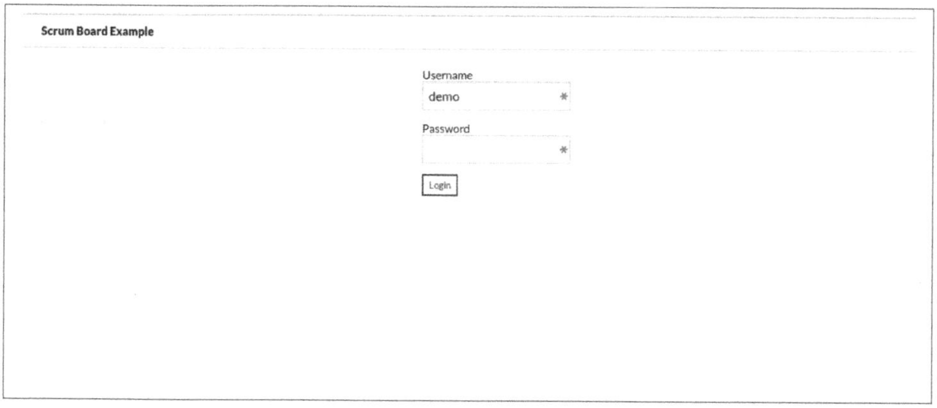

Figure 5-3. Welcome home page

After the form is submitted, the page should render the welcome message with the new header as in Figure 5-4.

Figure 5-4. Welcome home page with header

Now that the client can handle authentication with the API, the home page can be changed from a static welcome page to a dynamic application. Reviewing the preceding *index.html*, you can see how this project structure has created a good separation of client and server. There is no Django templating here other than the `static` and `url` usage, which could easily be replaced with the path references. This could also be output as static HTML as part of a build process similar to the project in Chapter 3, compressing and minifying the CSS and JavaScript as well.

Remember that the approach here is not unique to Backbone; much of the same techniques for defining configuration and code organization could be applied to frameworks such as Angular or Ember. In the next chapter, we'll continue walking through creating our Backbone application and exploring the unique experience of creating a single-page web application.

CHAPTER 6

Single-Page Web Application

Designing enriching experiences for the Web is something that we, as developers, consistently strive for. In recent years we have grown accustomed to combining different languages and frameworks, which usually requires better communication between the client-side and backend infrastructures.

With the recent shift in focus to client-side-heavy development, we're likely to pay even greater attention to the organization and structure of how we lay out the architecture of our projects. In this chapter, we'll create a simple single-page web application and step through how the Django framework fits into this new shift in development.

What Are Single-Page Web Applications?

Single-page web applications—SPAs—are a big part of this shift to client-side development. There are a few misconceptions as to what they are and how they should be used. Some developers believe that this category of applications includes only those that just need a single page, such as a to-do application. It's a reasonable assumption, but that is not entirely what the term "single page" means with these types of applications.

The "single page" part of an SPA refers to the fact that the server sends the client all of the presentation logic needed to a single page. From this starting point, the browser manipulates the data to create pages asynchronously and on an "as needed" basis. After this initial page load, the server interacts with the client over the API, sending only data on the wire. This reduces the response size and improves the cachability for each subsequent request. Since the entire page does not have to be refreshed by the browser, this architecture can create interfaces that quickly respond to user interactions.

You can see how this misconception might make some Django developers feel that SPAs are not malleable to their projects' needs. In this chapter, we'll focus on how to use the JSON data structures provided by our REST API from Chapter 4, and combine this with the basic layout and infrastructure from Chapter 5.

Discovering the API

Interactions with the API are handled through Backbone models and collections. These concepts map fairly closely to Django models and querysets.

Fetching the API

So far we've configured API root location using the django-rest-framework, but none of the subresources within our API. While we could use the same method to configure the locations for the sprints, tasks, and user endpoints, this wouldn't take advantage of the discoverability of the API itself. Instead we'll fetch the URLs for the available resources from the API root in our *models.js* file (located in *board/static/board/js*).

```
(function ($, Backbone, _, app) {
    ...
    app.models.Sprint = Backbone.Model.extend({});              ❶
    app.models.Task = Backbone.Model.extend({});
    app.models.User = Backbone.Model.extend({});

    app.collections.ready = $.getJSON(app.apiRoot);             ❷
    app.collections.ready.done(function (data) {                ❸
        app.collections.Sprints = Backbone.Collection.extend({
            model: app.models.Sprint,
            url: data.sprints
        });
        app.sprints = new app.collections.Sprints();
        app.collections.Tasks = Backbone.Collection.extend({
            model: app.models.Task,
            url: data.tasks
        });
        app.tasks = new app.collections.Tasks();
        app.collections.Users = Backbone.Collection.extend({
            model: app.models.User,
            url: data.users
        });
        app.users = new app.collections.Users();
    });

})(jQuery, Backbone, _, app);
```

❶ Create stubs for each of the models we will need: Sprint, Tasks, and User. Each is added to the app.models mapping to be used throughout the application.

❷ The API root is fetched and the AJAX deferred object is stored as app.collections.ready. This will allow other parts of the application to wait until the collections are ready.

❸ When the response comes back, the resulting URLs are used to build each of the collections. The collection definitions are added to the `app.collections` mapping, and shared instances of the collections are created as `app.sprints`, `app.tasks`, and `app.users`.

For now, these models and collections have no customizations from the Backbone defaults. We'll need to make a few changes to make this work better with `django-rest-framework` and our API by creating custom models with Backbone.

Model Customizations

In Backbone, the model URL will be constructed from the collections URL and by default does not include the trailing slash. While this is a normal pattern for the Java-Script framework, the `django-rest-framework` expects a trailing slash to be appended to the URL. We'll need to somehow incorporate that into our URL structure.

Also, the API will return the URL for the model in the `links` value. If this value is known, it should be used rather than constructing the URL. See the following snippet from *board/static/board/js/models.js.*

```
...
var BaseModel = Backbone.Model.extend({
    url: function () {                                          ❶
        var links = this.get('links'),
            url = links && links.self;
        if (!url) {
            url = Backbone.Model.prototype.url.call(this);     ❷
        }
        return url;
    }
});

app.models.Sprint = BaseModel.extend({});                      ❸
app.models.Task = BaseModel.extend({});
app.models.User = BaseModel.extend({});
...
```

❶ This code overrides the default URL construction and starts by looking for the `self` value from the `links` attribute.

❷ If the URL wasn't given by the API, it is constructed using the original Backbone method.

❸ The models have been changed to extend from `BaseModel` rather than `Backbone.Model`.

As mentioned, the default `Backbone.Model.url` constucts URLs without trailing slashes. However, `django-rest-framework` includes the trailing slash by default. Most of the time we are going to be using the URL returned by the API, but we still need to clean up this inconsistency for any place where the URL is constructed on the client from the base URL and the model id. Changing this on the server is straightfoward; we simply change the trailing_slash option when the router is constructed. We could also handle this by adding the trailing slash BaseModel.url function in *board/urls.py*.

```
from rest_framework.routers import DefaultRouter

from . import views


router = DefaultRouter(trailing_slash=False)
router.register(r'sprints', views.SprintViewSet)
router.register(r'tasks', views.TaskViewSet)
router.register(r'users', views.UserViewSet)
```

The API also expects the users to be referenced by username rather than id. We can configure this using the idAttribute model option in *board/static/board/js/models.js*.

```
...
app.models.User = BaseModel.extend({
    idAttributemodel: 'username'
});
...
```

As with our TemplateView and FormView, we now have a generic way to extend and further customize our application.

Collection Customizations

By default, Backbone expects all of the models to be listed as an array in our API response. The pagination implemented by the API wraps the list of objects with metadata about the pages and total counts. To get this to work with Backbone, we need to change the parse method on each collection. As with the models, this can be handled with a base collection class in *board/static/board/js/models.js*.

```
...
var BaseCollection = Backbone.Collection.extend({
    parse: function (response) {                                    ❶
        this._next = response.next;
        this._previous = response.previous;
        this._count = response.count;
        return response.results || [];
    }
});

app.collections.ready = $.getJSON(app.apiRoot);
app.collections.ready.done(function (data) {
    app.collections.Sprints = BaseCollection.extend({              ❷
        model: app.models.Sprint,
```

```
            url: data.sprints
        });
        app.sprints = new app.collections.Sprints();
        app.collections.Tasks = BaseCollection.extend({          ❸
            model: app.models.Task,
            url: data.tasks
        });
        app.tasks = new app.collections.Tasks();
        app.collections.Users = BaseCollection.extend({          ❹
            model: app.models.User,
            url: data.users
        });
        app.users = new app.collections.Users();
    });
    ...
```

❶   The `parse` override stores the `next`, `previous`, and `count` metadata on the collection and then returns the object list, which comes from the API `results` key.

❷ ❸   All the collections have been configured to extend from our `BaseCollection`.
❹

 This is a minimal approach to handling the API pagination. For a more comprehensive approach, take a look at backbone-paginator (*https://github.com/backbone-paginator/backbone.paginator*).

With all of this in place, we are ready to start using these models with our views.

Building Our Home Page

The home page will serve two purposes for our application: it should render the current sprints and allow for creating new ones. We'll start out by rendering the current sprints to be viewed once a user has been authenticated and redirected to the home page.

Displaying the Current Sprints

Let's review the current `HomepageView` from *views.js* (under *board/static/board/js*) that we recently created.

```
...
var HomepageView = TemplateView.extend({
    templateName: '#home-template'
});
...
```

As you can see, this renders the home-template with no additional context. The template needs to be passed the set of current sprints to be displayed on the page.

```
...
var HomepageView = TemplateView.extend({
    templateName: '#home-template',
    initialize: function (options) {                                    ❶
        var self = this;
        TemplateView.prototype.initialize.apply(this, arguments);
        app.collections.ready.done(function () {
            var end = new Date();
            end.setDate(end.getDate() - 7);
            end = end.toISOString().replace(/T.*/g, '');
            app.sprints.fetch({
                data: {end_min: end},
                success: $.proxy(self.render, self)
            });
        });
    },
    getContext: function () {
        return {sprints: app.sprints || null};                          ❷
    }
});
...
```

❶ When the view is created, sprints that have an end date greater than seven days ago are fetched. When the sprints are available, the view is rendered again to display them.

❷ The template context now contains the current sprints from app.sprints. This may be undefined if app.collections is not ready. In that case, the template will get a null value.

Our home page Underscore template (*board/templates/board/index.html*) now needs to be updated to handle both when the sprints are available and when they are still being loaded.

```
...
<script type="text/html" id="home-template">
    <h2>Your Sprints</h2>
    <button class="add" type="submit">Add Sprint</button>
    <% if (sprints !== null) { %>
        <div class="sprints">
            <% _.each(sprints.models, function (sprint) { %>          ❶
                <a href="#sprint/<%- sprint.get('id') %>" class="sprint">  ❷
                    <%- sprint.get('name') %> <br>
                    <span>DUE BY <%- sprint.get('end') %></span>
                </a>
            <% }); %>
        </div>
    <% } else { %>
        <h3 class="loading">Loading...</h3>                            ❸
    <% } %>
</script>
...
```

❶ When the sprints are not `null`, loop over and render the name and end date. The links are rendered to show the details for the sprint, but that route has not been added to the application yet and will be handled in a later section.

❸ A "Loading…" message displays if the sprints are `null`.

❷ The link will eventually navigate the user to see the details for the sprint. The application router currently doesn't handle links of this form; this will be updated later in the chapter.

We'll also add some CSS in *board/static/board/css/board.css* to implement some basic styling.

```
...
/* Sprint Listing
==================== */

.sprints {
    margin-top: 25px;
}

.sprints a.sprint {
    padding: 25px;
    float: left;
    text-align: center;
    background: #000;
    margin: 8px 8px 0 0;
    color: #FFF;
}

.sprints a.sprint span {
    font-size: 10px;
}
```

This is a complete rewrite of the original home page template that adds the dynamic data we want displayed for our application. As you can see, we've also included a button to add a new sprint. This is not currently functional, so let's implement that functionality in the next section.

Creating New Sprints

Part of any application development is creating a way for users to generate content. The home page does this by having a button that displays a form for the user to add new sprints. When that form is completed, it should also be removed.

The logic of creating new sprints will be handled by a subview to render the form. This can make use of the FormView, similar to the LoginView, as shown here in *board/static/board/js/views.js*.

```
...
var FormView = TemplateView.extend({
    ...
    modelFailure: function (model, xhr, options) {          ❶
        var errors = xhr.responseJSON;
        this.showErrors(errors);
    }
```

```
        });

        var NewSprintView = FormView.extend({                          ❷
            templateName: '#new-sprint-template',
            className: 'new-sprint',
            events: _.extend({                                         ❸
                'click button.cancel': 'done',
            }, FormView.prototype.events),
            submit: function (event) {
                var self = this,
                    attributes = {};
                FormView.prototype.submit.apply(this, arguments);
                attributes = this.serializeForm(this.form);
                app.collections.ready.done(function () {
                    app.sprints.create(attributes, {                  ❹
                        wait: true,
                        success: $.proxy(self.success, self),
                        error: $.proxy(self.modelFailure, self)       ❺
                    });
                });
            },
            success: function (model) {                               ❻
                this.done();
                window.location.hash = '#sprint/' + model.get('id');
            }
        });

        var HomepageView = TemplateView.extend({                      ❼
        ...
```

❷ ❼　This view extends the FormView helper and should be defined just before the HomepageView.

❸　Clicking the add button will trigger the form submit, which is handled by the FormView base. In addition to the default submit event handler, the view will also handle a cancel button to call the done method defined by the FormView.

❹　As with the LoginView, the form values are serialized. Instead of calling $.post manually, the view uses the app.sprints.create. The success and failure handlers are bound back to the view.

❻　When the sprint is created, the view calls done and redirects to the detail route for the sprint, which hasn't been written yet.

❶ ❺　The failure callback goes to a new modelFailure added to FormView. This is needed because while the $.ajax failure callback has the response object as the first argument, the Model.save has the model instance as the first argument and the response as the second.

Now we can create a template for the view in *board/templates/board/index.html* to include this form.

```
...
<script type="text/html" id="new-sprint-template">
    <form action="" method="post">
        <label for="id_name">Sprint Name</label>
        <input id="id_name" type="text" name="name" maxlength="100" required />
        <label for="id_end">End Date</label>
        <input id="id_end" type="date" name="end" />
        <label for="id_description">Description</label>
        <textarea id="id_description" name="description" cols="50"></textarea>
        <button class="cancel">Cancel</button>
        <button type="submit">Create</button>
    </form>
</script>
</head>
...
```

We have a view and template in place, but nothing yet to render them. This rendering is handled by the HomepageView (in *board/static/board/js/views.js*), which will add events that bind to a custom method.

```
...
var HomepageView = TemplateView.extend({
    templateName: '#home-template',
    events: {
        'click button.add': 'renderAddForm'                          ❶
    },
    initialize: function (options) {
        var self = this;
        TemplateView.prototype.initialize.apply(this, arguments);
        app.collections.ready.done(function () {
            var end = new Date();
            end.setDate(end.getDate() - 7);
            end = end.toISOString().replace(/T.*/g, '');
            app.sprints.fetch({
                data: {end_min: end},
                success: $.proxy(self.render, self)
            });
        });
    },
    getContext: function () {
        return {sprints: app.sprints || null};
    },
    renderAddForm: function (event) {                                ❷
        var view = new NewSprintView(),
            link = $(event.currentTarget);
        event.preventDefault();
        link.before(view.el);
        link.hide();
        view.render();
        view.on('done', function () {
            link.show();
        });
    });
```

```
        }
    });
    ...
```

❶ ❷ The click event for the add button is now handled by a renderAddForm. This creates a NewSprintView instance, which is rendered just above the button. When the view is done, either from the add or the cancel button, the link is shown again.

Now we need a little more CSS to clearly define the form from the listing, as shown here in *board/static/board/css/board.css*.

```
...
.new-sprint {
    border: 1px solid #CCC;
    padding: 20px;
}
```

When a new sprint is created, it will direct the user to #sprint/<id>, but nothing yet handles that route. Now it's time to move on to the detail page to display the data associated with each sprint.

Sprint Detail Page

The home page has given you a taste of composing a Backbone application with some basic model interactions, routes, views, and subviews. The sprint detail page is going to push this much further. Let's take a moment to review what we are planning on building for this page.

When viewing a sprint, we'll want to show the details of the sprint: name, end date, and description. There also should be columns for each status for the tasks assigned to the sprint. There will also be a listing for unassigned "backlog" tasks and where new ones can be created. A brief summary of each task will be shown, with more details available when the user clicks on the task.

With all of this sketched out, we'll start by rendering the sprint in a new view called SprintView.

Rendering the Sprint

To start rendering the data for our sprint detail page, we'll need to do a few things. We'll need a way to fetch the sprint data from our API and pass it into a template to render the details. Let's build out our view in *board/static/board/js/views.js* to point to this new template and pass in that data.

```
    ...
    var SprintView = TemplateView.extend({                              ❶
        templateName: '#sprint-template',
```

```
        initialize: function (options) {
            var self = this;
            TemplateView.prototype.initialize.apply(this, arguments);
            this.sprintId = options.sprintId;                              ❷
            this.sprint = null;
            app.collections.ready.done(function () {
                self.sprint = app.sprints.push({id: self.sprintId});       ❸
                self.sprint.fetch({
                    success: function () {
                        self.render();
                    }
                });
            });
        },
        getContext: function () {
            return {sprint: this.sprint};
        }
    });

    app.views.HomepageView = HomepageView;
    app.views.LoginView = LoginView;
    app.views.HeaderView = HeaderView;
    app.views.SprintView = SprintView;                                     ❹
    ...
```

❶ This extends from the `TemplateView` to make use of the existing hooks.

❷ ❸ `app.sprints.push` will put a new model instance into the client-site collection.
This model will know only the `id` of the model. The subsequent `fetch` will
retrieve the remaining details from the API.

❹ `SprintView` needs to be added to the `app.views` so that it can be used by the
router.

The sprint is fetched from the API when the view is initialized, and when it is available,
the view renders itself again. The view expects to be passed a `sprintId` when it is created
so that it knows which sprint to fetch. Before the view can be added to the router, the
`sprint-template` needs to be added to our *index.html* file (in *board/templates/board*).

```
    ...
    <script type="text/html" id="sprint-template">
        <% if (sprint !== null) { %>
            <h2><%- sprint.get('name') %></h2>
            <span class="due-date">Due <%- sprint.get('end') %></span>
            <p class="description"><%- sprint.get('description') %></p>
            <div class="tasks"></div>
        <% } else { %>
            <h1 class="loading">Loading...</h1>
        <% } %>
    </script>
```

```
</head>
  ...
```

Similar to the home page template, we've created a conditional statement to handle the several conditions on the sprint: if the sprint exists, if the sprint does not exist, and if the sprint is loading from the API itself. By using Underscore templates and basic JavaScript, we have created a dynamic way to easily display different states of this data.

Now we can add the view to the router and create the URL in which our sprint detail page is to be served.

Routing the Sprint Detail

As mentioned previously, our new `SprintView` requires the `sprintId` when it is created. This value will need to be captured from the route and passed to the view. As with Django, Backbone allows capturing parts of the route, but the syntax is slightly different. Let's add the route to the sprint detail page in our *router.js* file (located in *board/static/ board/js*).

```
...
var AppRouter = Backbone.Router.extend({
    routes: {
        '': 'home',
        'sprint/:id': 'sprint'                                      ❶
    },
    ...
    sprint: function (id) {                                         ❷
        var view = new app.views.SprintView({
            el: this.contentElement,
            sprintId: id
        });
        this.render(view);
    },
    route: function (route, name, callback) {
        ...
});
...
```

❶   A new entry is added to the `routes` configuration that maps to the `sprint` callback. This captures the value after the slash and passes it as `id` to the callback function. This matches the convention used previously in the home page template and in `NewSprintView`.

❷   The `sprint` callback takes the `id` and constructs a new `SprintView` and renders it.

You can see the minimal details of a sprint on the sprint detail URL, but you can't see any related tasks. One problem with this view is that it doesn't take advantage of state on the client, which is an important factor of this application. Let's review these client states and how to utilize them during this portion of the process.

Using the Client State

This first pass at fetching and rendering our sprint data is very much in line with what would be written onto the server. There are a few things to consider when we are working with dynamic and stateless data. Requests to the server are stateless and all the states needed are to be queried from the datastore. However, on the client we don't need to hit the API every time we need our model object—in this case, our sprint data.

It's possible that the sprint is already in the app.sprints collection. We can address this with a simple collection helper in *board/static/board/js/models.js*.

```
...
var BaseCollection = Backbone.Collection.extend({
    parse: function (response) {
        this._next = response.next;
        this._previous = response.previous;
        this._count = response.count;
        return response.results || [];
    },
    getOrFetch: function (id) {                                    ❶
        var result = new $.Deferred(),
            model = this.get(id);                                 ❷
        if (!model) {
            model = this.push({id: id});                          ❸
            model.fetch({
                success: function (model, response, options) {
                    result.resolve(model);
                },
                error: function (model, response, options) {
                    result.reject(model, response);
                }
            });
        } else {
            result.resolve(model);
        }
        return result;
    }
});
...
```

❶ This adds a new getOrFetch method to the BaseCollection. It returns a deferred object, which will resolve to the model instance.

❷   We look for the model in the current collection by its ID using this.get. Calling this.get does not make a request to the API server; it only looks for a model matching the given ID in the current in-memory list of models in the collection. If the model is found in the collection, the deferred object is immediately resolved with the result.

❸   If the model wasn't in the collection, it is fetched from the API. This step uses the same logic from the original view implementation, which first puts the empty model into the collection and retrieves it from the API.

The SprintView can now be updated in *board/static/board/js/views.js* to use this new method. It will need to handle both the successful case when the sprint is found, either locally or from the API, and the failure case when the sprint doesn't exist for the given sprintId.

```
...
var SprintView = TemplateView.extend({
    templateName: '#sprint-template',
    initialize: function (options) {
        var self = this;
        TemplateView.prototype.initialize.apply(this, arguments);
        this.sprintId = options.sprintId;
        this.sprint = null;
        app.collections.ready.done(function () {
            app.sprints.getOrFetch(self.sprintId).done(function (sprint) {   ❶
                self.sprint = sprint;
                self.render();
            }).fail(function (sprint) {                                      ❷
                self.sprint = sprint;
                self.sprint.invalid = true;
                self.render();
            });
        });
    },
    getContext: function () {
        return {sprint: this.sprint};
    }
});
...
```

❶   The original model, fetch, has been replaced by getOrFetch. Since it returns a deferred object, it has to be chained with a done callback for when the sprint is available.

❷   If fetching the model from the API raises an error, the fail callback will be fired. In this case we denote the sprint as invalid before rendering the template.

The fail handler takes into account a problem the previous code wasn't addressing: what if no sprint exists for the given id? Our final step to complete this improvement

is to update the template (*board/templates/board/index.html*) to handle the invalid sprint case.

```
...
<script type="text/html" id="sprint-template">
    <% if (sprint !== null) { %>
        <% if (!sprint.invalid) { %>                                ❶
            <h2><%- sprint.get('name') %></h2>
            <span class="due-date">Due <%- sprint.get('end') %></span>
            <p class="description"><%- sprint.get('description') %></p>
            <div class="tasks"></div>
        <% } else { %>                                              ❷
            <h1>Sprint <%- sprint.get('id') %> not found.</h1>
        <% } %>
    <% } else { %>
        <h1 class="loading">Loading...</h1>
    <% } %>
</script>
</head>
...
```

❶   New check to see if the sprint has the `invalid` flag set.

❷   If the sprint is marked as invalid, we'll add a simple message to let the user know.

The home page should now render the current sprints, as shown in Figure 6-1.

Figure 6-1. Sprint home page

With this improvement, the user can call a sprint link from the home page to see the sprint detail without initiating another API call. Next we'll start rendering the tasks that users will want to associate with each sprint.

Rendering the Tasks

In the current data model, tasks will most likely be assigned to a sprint in one of four statuses: not started, in development, in testing, and completed. A task can also exist even when it isn't yet associated with a sprint. In this application we want to display these task states as five different columns. Let's start with the view, which will handle one of these columns, in *board/static/board/js/views.js*.

```javascript
...
var StatusView = TemplateView.extend({
    tagName: 'section',
    className: 'status',
    templateName: '#status-template',
    initialize: function (options) {
        TemplateView.prototype.initialize.apply(this, arguments);
        this.sprint = options.sprint;
        this.status = options.status;
        this.title = options.title;
    },
    getContext: function () {
        return {sprint: this.sprint, title: this.title};
    }
});

var SprintView = TemplateView.extend({
...
```

This isn't much different from the other views we've based on `TemplateView`. It does expect three options to be defined: `sprint`, `status`, and `title`. The basic template needs to be added to *board/templates/board/index.html*.

```html
...
<script type="text/html" id="status-template">
    <h4><%- title %></h4>
    <div class="list"></div>
    <% if (sprint === null) { %>
        <button class="add" type="submit">Add Task</button>
    <% } %>
</script>
</head>
...
```

As mentioned previously, there will be a total of five instances of the `StatusView`. Those will be managed by the `SprintView` and should be implemented in *board/static/board/js/views.js* once the view has been initialized.

```javascript
...
var SprintView = TemplateView.extend({
    templateName: '#sprint-template',
    initialize: function (options) {
        var self = this;
        TemplateView.prototype.initialize.apply(this, arguments);
        this.sprintId = options.sprintId;
        this.sprint = null;
        this.statuses = {                                    ❶
            unassigned: new StatusView({
```

```
                       sprint: null, status: 1, title: 'Backlog'}),
                 todo: new StatusView({
                     sprint: this.sprintId, status: 1, title: 'Not Started'}),
                 active: new StatusView({
                     sprint: this.sprintId, status: 2, title: 'In Development'}),
                 testing: new StatusView({
                     sprint: this.sprintId, status: 3, title: 'In Testing'}),
                 done: new StatusView({
                     sprint: this.sprintId, status: 4, title: 'Completed'})
            };
            app.collections.ready.done(function () {
                app.sprints.getOrFetch(self.sprintId).done(function (sprint) {
                    self.sprint = sprint;
                    self.render();
                }).fail(function (sprint) {
                    self.sprint = sprint;
                    self.sprint.invalid = true;
                    self.render();
                });
            });
        },
        getContext: function () {
            return {sprint: this.sprint};
        },
        render: function () {                                              ❷
            TemplateView.prototype.render.apply(this, arguments);
            _.each(this.statuses, function (view, name) {
                $('.tasks', this.$el).append(view.el);
                view.delegateEvents();
                view.render();
            }, this);
        }
    });
    ...
```

❶ When the `SprintView` is created, a `StatusView` is created for each of the possible status cases.

❷ Rendering the `SprintView` will remove the existing elements for the subviews. The subviews will need to be reinserted into the DOM and the events will need to be bound again.

Even with these updates, this will only render the column headers since nothing yet fetches the tasks for each sprint. To handle this, we'll need to add two helper methods in *board/static/board/js/models.js*.

```
    ...
    app.models.Sprint = BaseModel.extend({
        fetchTasks: function () {                                          ❶
            var links = this.get('links');
            if (links && links.tasks) {
```

```
            app.tasks.fetch({url: links.tasks, remove: false});
        }
    }
});
...
app.collections.ready.done(function (data) {
    ...
    app.collections.Tasks = BaseCollection.extend({
        model: app.models.Task,
        url: data.tasks,
        getBacklog: function () {                                        ❷
            this.fetch({remove: false, data: {backlog: 'True'}});
        }
    });
    ...
});
...
```

❶ The first helper is `fetchTasks` on the `Sprint` model. It uses the `tasks` link given
    by the API. When this fetch is complete, the tasks will be added to the global
    `app.tasks` collection.

❷ The second helper is `getBacklog` on the `Tasks` collection. This uses the
    `backlog=True` filter to get tasks that aren't assigned to a sprint. Like `fetch`
    `Tasks`, the resulting tasks will be added to the global `app.tasks` collection.

Neither of these methods returns anything. Instead, the application will make use of the
events triggered by the `app.tasks` collection when these items are added. This will also
be handled by the `SprintView` in *board/static/board/js/views.js*.

```
...
var SprintView = TemplateView.extend({
    templateName: '#sprint-template',
    initialize: function (options) {
        var self = this;
        TemplateView.prototype.initialize.apply(this, arguments);
        this.sprintId = options.sprintId;
        this.sprint = null;
        this.statuses = {
            unassigned: new StatusView({
                sprint: null, status: 1, title: 'Backlog'}),
            todo: new StatusView({
                sprint: this.sprintId, status: 1, title: 'Not Started'}),
            active: new StatusView({
                sprint: this.sprintId, status: 2, title: 'In Development'}),
            testing: new StatusView({
                sprint: this.sprintId, status: 3, title: 'In Testing'}),
            done: new StatusView({
                sprint: this.sprintId, status: 4, title: 'Completed'})
        };
        app.collections.ready.done(function () {
```

```
        app.tasks.on('add', self.addTask, self);                    ❶
        app.sprints.getOrFetch(self.sprintId).done(function (sprint) {
            self.sprint = sprint;
            self.render();
            // Add any current tasks
            app.tasks.each(self.addTask, self);                      ❷
            // Fetch tasks for the current sprint
            sprint.fetchTasks();                                     ❸
        }).fail(function (sprint) {
            self.sprint = sprint;
            self.sprint.invalid = true;
            self.render();
        });
        // Fetch unassigned tasks
        app.tasks.getBacklog();                                      ❹
    });
    },
    getContext: function () {
        return {sprint: this.sprint};
    },
    render: function () {
        TemplateView.prototype.render.apply(this, arguments);
        _.each(this.statuses, function (view, name) {
            $('.tasks', this.$el).append(view.el);
            view.delegateEvents();
            view.render();
        }, this);
    },
    addTask: function (task) {
        // TODO: Handle the task
    }
});
...
```

❸❹ When the collection is ready, the backlog tasks can be fetched; and when the
      sprint has been fetched, the related tasks can be fetched.

❶   As the results are returned, app.tasks will fire the add event, which will be
      bound to addTask on the view.

❷   It's possible that there are already tasks stored on the client if we have navigated
      between sprint pages. Those need to be added as well. Keep in mind that not all
      the tasks will be relevant for this sprint, and they'll also need to be filtered out
      in the addTask callback.

The addTask callback will handle tasks received from the API as well as those that were
already available on the client. The task should be rendered only if it is either related to
the sprint or a backlog task. Where it will be rendered will depend on the sprint and
status of the task. Let's add some new methods to the Task model in *board/static/board/
js/models.js* to help sort out this logic.

```
...
app.models.Task = BaseModel.extend({
    statusClass: function () {                                              ❶
        var sprint = this.get('sprint'),
            status;
        if (!sprint) {
            status = 'unassigned';
        } else {
            status = ['todo', 'active', 'testing', 'done'][this.get('status') - 1];
        }
        return status;
    },
    inBacklog: function () {                                                ❷
        return !this.get('sprint');
    },
    inSprint: function (sprint) {                                           ❸
        return sprint.get('id') == this.get('sprint');
    }
});
...
```

❶   statusClass helps map the task to the StatusView to which it should be associated.

❷   inBacklog determines what it means for the task to be on the backlog.

❸   inSprint determines if the task is in the given sprint.

Now we can return to the SprintView in *board/static/board/js/views.js* to handle adding the task.

```
...
var SprintView = TemplateView.extend({
    templateName: '#sprint-template',
    initialize: function (options) {
        var self = this;
        TemplateView.prototype.initialize.apply(this, arguments);
        this.sprintId = options.sprintId;
        this.sprint = null;
        this.tasks = [];                                                   ❶
        this.statuses = {
            unassigned: new StatusView({
                sprint: null, status: 1, title: 'Backlog'}),
            todo: new StatusView({
                sprint: this.sprintId, status: 1, title: 'Not Started'}),
            active: new StatusView({
                sprint: this.sprintId, status: 2, title: 'In Development'}),
            testing: new StatusView({
                sprint: this.sprintId, status: 3, title: 'In Testing'}),
            done: new StatusView({
                sprint: this.sprintId, status: 4, title: 'Completed'})
        };
```

```
        app.collections.ready.done(function () {
            app.tasks.on('add', self.addTask, self);
            app.sprints.getOrFetch(self.sprintId).done(function (sprint) {
                self.sprint = sprint;
                self.render();
                // Add any current tasks
                app.tasks.each(self.addTask, self);
                // Fetch tasks for the current sprint
                sprint.fetchTasks();
            }).fail(function (sprint) {
                self.sprint = sprint;
                self.sprint.invalid = true;
                self.render();
            });
            // Fetch unassigned tasks
            app.tasks.getBacklog();
        });
    },
    getContext: function () {
        return {sprint: this.sprint};
    },
    render: function () {
        TemplateView.prototype.render.apply(this, arguments);
        _.each(this.statuses, function (view, name) {
            $('.tasks', this.$el).append(view.el);
            view.delegateEvents();
            view.render();
        }, this);
        _.each(this.tasks, function (task) {                          ❷
            this.renderTask(task);
        }, this);
    },
    addTask: function (task) {                                       ❸
        if (task.inBacklog() || task.inSprint(this.sprint)) {
            this.tasks[task.get('id')] = task;
            this.renderTask(task);
        }
    },
    renderTask: function (task) {                                    ❹
        var column = task.statusClass(),
            container = this.statuses[column],
            html = _.template('<div><%- task.get("name") %></div>', {task: task});
        $('.list', container.$el).append(html);
    }
});
...
```

❶ ❸ addTask now filters tasks to those relevant for this view. It also holds a list of all of the added tasks in case the view needs to be rendered again.

❷ ❹ Rendering the tasks is currently handled by an inline Underscore template. This will later be refactored into its own subview and template.

With our `SprintView` in place and offering us a way to handle working with tasks associated with it, we can begin writing all of the components to build out our task views.

AddTaskView

Enabling users to generate tasks and assign them to a sprint is the core part of our Scrum board application. We'll need to not only build out our models, views, and templates, but also think about all of the different ways in which we manage that data.

Before we do that, let's add a simple `AddTaskView` to *board/static/board/js/views.js* to create a way for users to add a task to a sprint.

```
...
var AddTaskView = FormView.extend({                         ❶
    templateName: '#new-task-template',
    events: _.extend({
        'click button.cancel': 'done'
    }, FormView.prototype.events),
    submit: function (event) {
        var self = this,
            attributes = {};
        FormView.prototype.submit.apply(this, arguments);
        attributes = this.serializeForm(this.form);         ❷
        app.collections.ready.done(function () {
            app.tasks.create(attributes, {                  ❸
                wait: true,
                success: $.proxy(self.success, self),
                error: $.proxy(self.modelFailure, self)
            });
        });
    },
    success: function (model, resp, options) {
        this.done();
    }
});

var StatusView = TemplateView.extend({
...
```

❶ We'll be extending our `FormView` to implement the basic template rendering and form submission and error handling.

❷ The code serializes the form into digestible JSON data that our API can consume.

❸ Here we create the new tasks inside the collection and assign the various attributes for interactions with the API. Because we are using the model `save`, the failure is bound to the `modelFailure` callback from the `FormView`.

As with `NewSprintView`, this view adds a new event handler to handle the cancel button. Let's make this the default in the `FormView` (in *board/static/board/js/views.js*).

```
...
var FormView = TemplateView.extend({
    events: {
        'submit form': 'submit',
        'click button.cancel': 'done'                            ❶
    },
    ...
});
...
var NewSprintView = FormView.extend({
    templateName: '#new-sprint-template',
    className: 'new-sprint',                                     ❷
    ...
});
...
var AddTaskView = FormView.extend({
    templateName: '#new-task-template',                         ❸
    ...
});
...
```

❶ FormView now binds any `button.cancel` click to the done method by default.

❷ ❸ NewSprintView and AddTaskView no longer need to extend the events, and this declaration can be removed from each view.

With that minor refactor complete, next we'll need to update our StatusView in *board/static/board/js/views.js* to render this new form.

```
...
var StatusView = TemplateView.extend({
    tagName: 'section',
    className: 'status',
    templateName: '#status-template',
    events: {
        'click button.add': 'renderAddForm'                     ❶
    },
    initialize: function (options) {
        TemplateView.prototype.initialize.apply(this, arguments);
        this.sprint = options.sprint;
        this.status = options.status;
        this.title = options.title;
    },
    getContext: function () {
        return {sprint: this.sprint, title: this.title};
    },
    renderAddForm: function (event) {                            ❷
        var view = new AddTaskView(),
            link = $(event.currentTarget);
        event.preventDefault();
        link.before(view.el);
        link.hide();
```

```
            view.render();
            view.on('done', function () {
                link.show();
            });
        }
    });
    ...
```

❶ The view now binds an event handler for clicking the button with an add class. While all instances of this view will have this handler, the only template that renders the button is the StatusView instance for the backlog tasks.

❷ Similar to how the home page adds sprints, a new AddTaskView instance is created when the button is clicked and removes itself when it is done, either from creating a new task or the user clicking cancel.

Now we can add our new-task-template into our *index.html* file (under *board/ templates/board*) to complete our task creation workflow.

```
...
<script type="text/html" id="new-task-template">
    <form class="add-task" action="" method="post">
        <label for="id_name">Task Name</label>
        <input id="id_name" type="text" name="name" maxlength="100" required />
        <label for="id_description">Description</label>
        <textarea id="id_description" name="description"></textarea>
        <button class="create" type="submit">Create</button>
        <button class="cancel" type="submit">Cancel</button>
    </form>
</script>
</head>
...
```

To give this page a more readable and usable structure, we'll add some CSS to *board/ static/board/css/board.css*.

```
...
/* Tasks
===================== */

.tasks {
    display: -webkit-box;
    display: -moz-box;
    display: -ms-flexbox;
    display: -webkit-flex;
    display: flex;

    -webkit-flex-flow: row wrap;

    align-items: strech;
    overflow: scroll;
}
```

```
.tasks .status {
    background: #EEE;
    border: 1px solid #CCC;
    padding: 0 10px 15px 10px;
    margin-right: 8px;
    width: 17%;
}

.tasks .status .list {
    display: -webkit-box;
    display: -moz-box;
    display: -ms-flexbox;
    display: -webkit-flex;
    display: flex;

    -webkit-flex-flow: row wrap;
    flex-direction: row;
    justify-content: space-around;
}

.task-detail input, .task-detail textarea {
    width: 90%;
}
```

We should add a few other ways for our users to interact with tasks to customize them at varying points of the process. Let's use the four different CRUD operations as a base for the interactions we'll be building.

CRUD Tasks

Being able to create editable content with Backbone while working with a custom API is a very powerful tool for developing enriching experiences with our web applications. At this point in our Scrum application, we have the ability to create a sprint and add a task to it. Now let's add a few more ways for us to interact with the data by leveraging the three other CRUD methods: read, update, and delete.

Rendering Tasks Within a Sprint

To start, we'll build a basic view that encompasses various aspects when rendering each task into our template. As in our `TaskView` creation, we'll need to refactor our `SprintView` code by removing the inline Underscore template and pointing our `ren derTask` method to this new view. Recall the current `SprintView.renderTask` method in *board/static/board/js/views.js*.

```
var SprintView = TemplateView.extend({
...
    renderTask: function (task) {
        var column = task.statusClass(),
```

```
                container = this.statuses[column],
                html = _.template('<div><%- task.get("name") %></div>', {task: task});
            $('.list', container.$el).append(html);
        }
    });
    ...
```

renderTask has two main problems to address. First, the inline template isn't consistent with how the other views manage templates, which will become a problem when we need to handle events for editing tasks. Second, renderTask injects this HTML inside an element that is rendered and controlled by one of the StatusView instances. It would be better to let the StatusView determine the best place for the task.

This inline template can easily be factored out into a template in the <head> of *board/ templates/board/index.html*, as with the other templates.

```
...
<script type="text/html" id="task-item-template">
    <%- task.get('name') %>
</script>
</head>
...
```

Next, we can create our TaskItemView in *board/static/board/js/views.js* to render each task using this template.

```
...
var TaskItemView = TemplateView.extend({
    tagName: 'div',
    className: 'task-item',
    templateName: '#task-item-template',
    initialize: function (options) {
        TemplateView.prototype.initialize.apply(this, arguments);
        this.task = options.task;
        this.task.on('change', this.render, this);
        this.task.on('remove', this.remove, this);
    },
    getContext: function () {
        return {task: this.task};
    },
    render: function () {
        TemplateView.prototype.render.apply(this, arguments);
        this.$el.css('order', this.task.get('order'));
    }
});

var SprintView = TemplateView.extend({
    ...
```

TaskItemView follows the pattern of most of the existing TemplateView examples with a few small differences. On initialize, it binds itself to the model's change and remove events. If the model instance is updated on the client, the view will render itself again to reflect those updates. If the model is deleted, the view will remove itself from the DOM. The render also sets the order CSS on the element, which is used by the flexbox layout to correctly render the order regardless of the position in the DOM.

Now that we have our basic view for displaying our tasks, we can use it in the SprintView.renderTask method in *board/static/board/js/views.js*.

```
...
var StatusView = TemplateView.extend({
    ...
    addTask: function (view) {                                    ❶
        $('.list', this.$el).append(view.el);
    }
});
...
var SprintView = TemplateView.extend({
    templateName: '#sprint-template',
    initialize: function (options) {
        var self = this;
        TemplateView.prototype.initialize.apply(this, arguments);
        this.sprintId = options.sprintId;
        this.sprint = null;
        this.tasks = {};                                         ❷
        this.statuses = {
            unassigned: new StatusView({
                sprint: null, status: 1, title: 'Backlog'}),
            todo: new StatusView({
                sprint: this.sprintId, status: 1, title: 'Not Started'}),
            active: new StatusView({
                sprint: this.sprintId, status: 2, title: 'In Development'}),
            testing: new StatusView({
                sprint: this.sprintId, status: 3, title: 'In Testing'}),
            done: new StatusView({
                sprint: this.sprintId, status: 4, title: 'Completed'})
        };
        app.collections.ready.done(function () {
            app.tasks.on('add', self.addTask, self);
            app.sprints.getOrFetch(self.sprintId).done(function (sprint) {
                self.sprint = sprint;
                self.render();
                // Add any current tasks
                app.tasks.each(self.addTask, self);
                // Fetch tasks for the current sprint
                sprint.fetchTasks();
            }).fail(function (sprint) {
                self.sprint = sprint;
                self.sprint.invalid = true;
                self.render();
            });
            // Fetch unassigned tasks
            app.tasks.getBacklog();
```

```
            });
        },
        getContext: function () {
            return {sprint: this.sprint};
        },
        render: function () {
            TemplateView.prototype.render.apply(this, arguments);
            _.each(this.statuses, function (view, name) {
                $('.tasks', this.$el).append(view.el);
                view.delegateEvents();
                view.render();
            }, this);
            _.each(this.tasks, function (view, taskId) {                          ❸
                var task = app.tasks.get(taskId);
                view.remove();
                this.tasks[taskId] = this.renderTask(task);
            }, this);
        },
        addTask: function (task) {
            if (task.inBacklog() || task.inSprint(this.sprint)) {
                this.tasks[task.get('id')] = this.renderTask(task);            ❹
            }
        },
        renderTask: function (task) {                                          ❺
            var view = new TaskItemView({task: task});
            _.each(this.statuses, function (container, name) {
                if (container.sprint == task.get('sprint') &&
                    container.status == task.get('status')) {
                    container.addTask(view);
                }
            });
            view.render();
            return view;
        }
    });
    ...
```

❶   StatusView has a new addTask method to add a task view, and it does the insert
    into the DOM.

❷ ❸ The tasks attribute has been changed from a list to an associative array, which
❹   maps the task.id to the subview instance for the task. addTask is updated for
    the assignment. render is updated to iterate over the mapping.

❺   renderTask creates an instance of the new TaskItemView and loops through the
    status subviews. renderTask now returns the subview, which is used by add
    Task to track the task to view mapping.

Here we add to *board/static/board/css/board.css* some minor style to space out the tasks.

```
    ...
    .tasks .task-item {
```

```
        width: 100%;
        margin: 5px 0;
        padding: 3px;
    }
```

The details for the first sprint, "Something Sprint," should match Figure 6-2.

Scrum Board Example				Your Sprints	Logout

Something Sprint

Due 2020-12-31

Test

Backlog	Not Started	In Development	In Testing	Completed
Add Task	First Task			

Figure 6-2. Sprint details

 This assumes you've followed along with the sprints and tasks as they were created and assigned while we explored the API in Chapter 4.

With this very minimal structure in place, we should now think about how the different aspects of a task are viewed by the user and the interactions that will need to happen on that view.

Updating Tasks

As tasks are an inherent part of building the content within a sprint, it is fairly important for users to be able to view and edit details within that task. Our process to implement this functionality will be similar to adding a task. When the user clicks on a task item, a form opens to show more detail about the task and allow for editing it. The user can save the changes or click cancel to close the form. Let's start by creating this detail view in *board/static/board/js/views.js*.

```
...
var TaskDetailView = FormView.extend({
    tagName: 'div',
    className: 'task-detail',
    templateName: '#task-detail-template',
    initialize: function (options) {                            ❶
```

```
            FormView.prototype.initialize.apply(this, arguments);
            this.task = options.task;
            this.changes = {};
            $('button.save', this.$el).hide();
            this.task.on('change', this.render, this);
            this.task.on('remove', this.remove, this);
        },
        getContext: function () {
            return {task: this.task, empty: '-----'};                ❷
        },
        submit: function (event) {
            FormView.prototype.submit.apply(this, arguments);
            this.task.save(this.changes, {                           ❸
                wait: true,
                success: $.proxy(this.success, this),
                error: $.proxy(this.modelFailure, this)
            });
        },
        success: function (model) {                                   ❹
            this.changes = {};
            $('button.save', this.$el).hide();
        }
    });

    var TaskItemView = TemplateView.extend({
    ...
```

❶   Similar to the smaller `TaskItemView`, the `TaskDetailView` listens for changes to the model. It also keeps track of any changes the user has made to the model.

❷   In addition to the task, the template will be rendered with "`-----`" as a value if there is no content associated with a particular attribute on the task.

❸ ❹   The form saves the changes made by the user. When the save is successful, those changes are reset.

Now we can add our task detail template to *board/templates/board/index.html* and include the corresponding form for creating a new task within a sprint.

```
    ...
    <script type="text/html" id="task-detail-template">
        <div data-field="name" class="name">
            <%- task.get('name') %>
        </div>
        <div data-field="description" class="description">
            <%- task.get('description') %>
        </div>
        <div class="with-label">
            <div class="label">Due:</div>
            <div data-field="due" class="due date">
                <%- task.get('due') || empty %>
            </div>
```

```
        </div>
        <div class="with-label">
            <div class="label">Assigned To:</div>
            <div data-field="assigned" class="assigned">
                <%- task.get('assigned') || empty %>
            </div>
        </div>
        <form>
            <button class="cancel" type="submit">Close</button>
            <button class="save" hidden type="submit">Save</button>
        </form>
    </script>
    </head>
    ...
```

The save button is hidden by default and will be shown only when there are changes to save. The TaskDetailView instances need to be created when the user clicks on a task in the listing. TaskItemView needs to listen for this event. Here is how we implement these requirements in *board/static/board/js/views.js*.

```
...
var TaskItemView = TemplateView.extend({
    tagName: 'div',
    className: 'task-item',
    templateName: '#task-item-template',
    events: {
        'click': 'details'                                              ❶
    },
    initialize: function (options) {
        TemplateView.prototype.initialize.apply(this, arguments);
        this.task = options.task;
        this.task.on('change', this.render, this);
        this.task.on('remove', this.remove, this);
    },
    getContext: function () {
        return {task: this.task};
    },
    render: function () {
        TemplateView.prototype.render.apply(this, arguments);
        this.$el.css('order', this.task.get('order'));
    },
    details: function () {                                              ❷
        var view = new TaskDetailView({task: this.task});
        this.$el.before(view.el);
        this.$el.hide();
        view.render();
        view.on('done', function () {
            this.$el.show();
        }, this);
    }
});
...
```

❶   `TaskItemView` now binds the `click` event to a new `details` callback.

❷   In the event callback, a new `TaskDetailView` instance is created for the task. The current view is hidden until the edit is complete, which is indicated by the done event fired by the `FormView`.

This will now expand the task details on click, and those details can be hidden again with the close button, but the task is not yet editable. Nothing in the view currently updates the `changes` that the view uses to track the model updates. This is what we'll address next.

Inline Edit Features

Being able to easily edit content while staying inline with the content you are editing is a critical component of easy-to-use experiences. Since we want to follow these types of patterns in our application and create these types of interactions with our users, let's add in the ability to create inline editable content by using a custom method on the `contenteditable` HTML5 element (in *board/static/board/js/views.js*).

```
...
var TaskDetailView = FormView.extend({
    tagName: 'div',
    className: 'task-detail',
    templateName: '#task-detail-template',
    events: _.extend({
        'blur [data-field][contenteditable=true]': 'editField'    ❶
    }, FormView.prototype.events),
...
    editField: function (event) {                                 ❷
        var $this = $(event.currentTarget),
            value = $this.text().replace(/^\s+|\s+$/g,''),
            field = $this.data('field');
        this.changes[field] = value;
        $('button.save', this.$el).show();
    }
});
...
```

❶   This code adds in the event listener to find all of the places in which `contenteditable` appears in our template.

❷   This is a custom method that makes the particular content fields available for editing and saving back to our API. Leading and trailing whitespace is removed from the text content.

With our new method in place, we can now add in our template (*board/templates/board/index.html*) and assign `contenteditable` to each section that we want to be editable inline. Particular areas of the DOM are associated with a model field via a data-field attribute.

```
...
<script type="text/html" id="task-detail-template">
    <div data-field="name" class="name" contenteditable="true">
        <%- task.get('name') %>
    </div>
    <div data-field="description" class="description" contenteditable="true">
        <%- task.get('description') %>
    </div>
    <div class="with-label">
        <div class="label">Due:</div>
        <div data-field="due" class="due date" contenteditable="true">
            <%- task.get('due') || empty %>
        </div>
    </div>
    <div class="with-label">
        <div class="label">Assigned To:</div>
        <div data-field="assigned" class="assigned" contenteditable="true">
            <%- task.get('assigned') || empty %>
        </div>
    </div>
    <form>
        <button class="cancel" type="submit">Close</button>
        <button class="save hide" type="submit">Save</button>
    </form>
</script>
</head>
...
```

One problem with this approach is that the default FormView.showErrors won't work to display the errors from the API. The FormView.showErrors relied on the <input> and <label> tags to have names matching the model names. These are not present in the current template. To address this, TaskDetailView needs to define its own showErrors that associates the errors with the correct areas based on the data-field attributes, as shown here in *board/static/board/js/views.js*.

```
var TaskDetailView = FormView.extend({
...
    showErrors: function (errors) {
        _.map(errors, function (fieldErrors, name) {
            var field = $('[data-field=' + name + ']', this.$el);
            if (field.length === 0) {
                field = $('[data-field]', this.$el).first();
            }
            function appendError(msg) {
                var parent = field.parent('.with-label'),
                    error = this.errorTemplate({msg: msg});
                if (parent.length === 0) {
                    field.before(error);
```

```
                } else {
                    parent.before(error);
                }
            }
            _.map(fieldErrors, appendError, this);
        }, this);
    }
});
```

We need additional styles in *board/static/board/css/board.css* to make the detail/edit state more distinct from the normal listing.

```
...
/* Task Detail
==================== */
.task-detail {
    width: 100%;
    margin: 5px 0;
    background-color: #FFF;
    padding: 8px;
}

.task-detail div {
    margin-bottom: 10px;
}

.task-detail .name, .task-detail .description {
    border-bottom: 1px dotted #333;
}

.task-detail .with-label {
    display: -webkit-box;
    display: -moz-box;
    display: -ms-flexbox;
    display: -webkit-flex;
    display: flex;
}

[contenteditable=true]:hover {
    background: #EEE;
}

[contenteditable=true]:focus {
    background: #FFF;
}
```

We now have a fully functioning Backbone application with the ability to add sprints and tasks and edit them while working with our REST API. There is a clear separation of client and server, with minimal configuration passed between them. The JavaScript client discovers the API layout from the root and the links information provided by the resource responses. After the initial page load, the Django application sends only data over the wire. Since the payloads are small and focused, they are light on bandwidth (which is good for mobile devices) and easily cacheable (which is good for everyone). The interactions can be handled on the client without the round-trip to the server and full-page refresh, which creates a seamless experience for the user. While managing complex state on the client can be tricky, the Backbone views and models, along with the Underscore templates, provide a set of tools similar to Django to make this more manageable. In the following chapters, we'll be covering how to use websockets to create real-time effects with our data and provide an even more enriching experience.

CHAPTER 7

Real-Time Django

There has been a recent trend toward building real-time web applications or integrating real-time components into existing applications. However, Django is primarily optimized for short-lived HTTP request/response cycles, and most Python web servers are not made for handling a large number of concurrent and long-lived connections required to support real-time applications. The rise of Node.js and the inclusion of `asyncio` in the Python standard library have many developers using cooperative multitasking and event loops for a solution to the high-concurrency problem. However, this solution requires the entire stack to be written in this cooperative fashion to ensure that nothing blocks the loop. There is no easy way to make this drop into an existing Django application. Beyond inefficient long polling, there is no obvious solution to add real-time features to a Django application.

In this chapter, we'll explore how to integrate real-time features into the same task-board application backed by the Django-based REST API. The real-time features will be handled by a new server, written using Tornado, that uses asynchronous I/O to handle a large number of concurrent connections. We'll learn how to effectively and securely allow Django to push updates to the client. First we'll examine the set of new web APIs defined in HTML5 to better understand this approach.

HTML5 Real-Time APIs

We will incorporate real-time updates to our application to let users see tasks moving status and changing order. For our application, the protocol for client updates is already well defined by the REST API. However, there are client updates that would be helpful to know but don't need to be stored, such as when a user starts to move a task. This will allow the application to notify other clients viewing the sprint for the task that another user is changing it. Since there is some bidirectionality to the client-server communication, we will implement this functionality with websockets.

The real-time Web has evolved from early approaches of long polling and Comet to new web standards in HTML5 including websockets, server-sent events (SSEs), and web real-time communication (WebRTC). Each of these fits different use cases and has different scaling needs and current browser support. Each can be made to work with a Django application using an approach similar to what we'll build in this chapter. Next we give a quick breakdown of the current state of real-time web APIs.

Websockets

Websockets are a specification for a two-way communication between the browser and the server. This connection is persistent, which means the server must be able to handle a large number of open connections at once. Care must be taken in the server as well that connections don't use other resources that might be limited. For instance, if each web server connection opens a connection to a database, then the number of connections will be limited not necessarily by the amount of connections the webserver can hold, but instead by the number of connections at the database. Websockets are the most commonly known of the HTML5 standards and have the best browser support. The latest versions of the most popular desktop browsers all support websockets. Support is improving for mobile browsers.

> You can find an up-to-date breakdown of the current browser support for websockets at *http://caniuse.com/#feat=websockets*.

Server-Sent Events

Like websockets, server-sent events require a long-lived server connection. However, unlike websockets, this isn't a two-way connection. The server-sent event connection allows the server to push new events to the client. As you might expect, both the client- and server-side APIs are much simpler than the websocket protocol. You can handle any updates from the client by initiating a new HTTP request. Internet Explorer as of 11.0 does not have support for SSEs, but it is otherwise on a par with websocket support.

> You can find an up-to-date breakdown of the current browser support for server-sent events at *http://caniuse.com/#feat=eventsource*.

WebRTC

Unlike the previous two specifications, WebRTC is a browser-to-browser communication protocol. While a server is typically needed for the discovery of the other client and the initial handshakes, once the connection is established the server does not see the communication. Original support was for streaming audio and video channels between clients, but more recently there is support for sending arbitrary data. This fits a use case where clients need to sync a large amount of state between each other, which is not a concern of the server. WebRTC can be combined with the other protocols for real-time updates to and from the server as well as between the clients. This is the least mature of the HTML5 standards and has the least browser support, with both Internet Explorer 11.0 and Safari 8.0 lacking it. Mobile support is also largely nonexistent.

You can find an up-to-date breakdown of the current browser support for WebRTC at *http://caniuse.com/#feat=rtcpeerconnection.*

Websockets with Tornado

We will write the websocket server itself using Tornado, which is an asynchronous network library and small web framework written in Python. It was originally developed at FriendFeed and continues to be maintained by Facebook after the acquisition. It runs on a single-threaded event loop based on select/epoll and can handle a large number of simultaneous connections with a small memory footprint. Both the core networking functionality and web framework are simple and readable, and there is solid documentation and examples. Currently, it has the most mature Python 3 support of the asynchronous Python frameworks.

You can read more about the features of Tornado and read the official documentation on the project website (*http://www.tornado web.org/*).

There are a few reasons why we don't just build all this into one Django server. First, Django is based primarily on the WSGI specification, which is not geared toward handling long-lived connections. Most WSGI servers handle large concurrency through multithreading, but this approach simply doesn't scale well to a large number of long-lived connections. I/O bound, multithreaded Python applications also occasionally run into issues with the Global Interpreter Lock (GIL).

Some have tried the approach of using lightweight or "green" threads in place of native threads. This approach has its advantages, but at its core it works much the same as the single-threaded event loop. It is cooperative multitasking. If there are pieces of the application that do not yield the event loop when doing I/O, then all connections are blocked. Implicit async frameworks, such as `gevent` and `eventlet`, monkey-patch I/O libraries in the Python standard library, such as the `socket` library. C extensions to Python that do network operations cannot be patched in this fashion. Tracking down bugs related to the loop being blocked in these implicit async frameworks can be difficult to debug as well as hard or impossible to work around.

Another reason to have a separate server for the websocket is a separation of concerns. Django expects connections to be short-lived, and in the case of this REST API, completely stateless. The websocket connections will be long-lived and potentially stateful. These lend themselves to having different scaling concerns. Also, the real-time features of this application are more nice-to-have than core to the functionality of the application. There may be cases where it isn't feasible or reasonable for the client to enable them, such as older browsers or underpowered mobile devices. By housing these connections in separate processes, the real-time server can fail and the core of the application can still be used. This requires the Django application and the real-time server to share as little as possible. All information that does need to be shared will be done through a well-defined API.

Tornado is not your only option for this server. The real-time server could be written in Node, Erlang, Haskell, or whatever language or framework seems best suited for the task. If implemented correctly, there should not be any changes to the Django side if it has been swapped out for a different language or framework later. The important part of this is the separation and the well-defined communication between the two servers.

Introduction to Tornado

As previously noted, we'll be using Tornado to build our real-time server component. Tornado can be installed from the PyPi using `pip`.

```
hostname $ pip install tornado
```

 As of version 3.2, Tornado includes an optional C extension that improves the performance of websocket connections. However, it requires a working C compiler to install. If a C compiler is found on the system at install time, it will build the extension automatically. Tornado 4.0 added `certifi` as a dependency.

For many web applications, you do not need to dive into the low-level networking pieces that Tornado provides and instead can focus on the web framework built into Tornado. The framework is built around two main classes: `RequestHandler` and `Application`.

The RequestHandler does exactly what its name implies and has an API similar to Django's View class, which is the base of all class-based views. Application doesn't map directly to any one concept in Django. It covers the same functionality as Django's root URL conf and Django's settings; that is, Application maps URLs to RequestHandler classes as well as handles global configurations or shared resources. Tornado has built-in support for handling websocket connections by subclassing tornado.websocket.WebSocketHandler.

The start of the Tornado server for handling updates to a given sprint, known as *watercooler.py*, will look like this:

```python
from urllib.parse import urlparse

from tornado.ioloop import IOLoop
from tornado.web import Application
from tornado.websocket import WebSocketHandler


class SprintHandler(WebSocketHandler):                              ❶
    """Handles real-time updates to the board."""

    def check_origin(self, origin):                                ❷
        allowed = super().check_origin(origin)
        parsed = urlparse(origin.lower())
        return allowed or parsed.netloc.startswith('localhost:')

    def open(self, sprint):
        """Subscribe to sprint updates on a new connection."""

    def on_message(self, message):
        """Broadcast updates to other interested clients."""

    def on_close(self):
        """Remove subscription."""


if __name__ == "__main__":
    application = Application([                                     ❸
        (r'/(?P<sprint>[0-9]+)', SprintHandler),
    ])
    application.listen(8080)
    IOLoop.instance().start()
```

❶ SprintHandler is the handler class for the websocket connection. The open, on_message, and on_close methods are the API defined by WebSocketHandler, which we will write to add the functionality we need.

❸ The Application is constructed with a single route to the websocket handler and configured to listen on port 8080.

❷ check_origin is overridden to allow cross-domain requests. For now it will allow connections from any server running locally. This will work for development, and we'll make it more configurable later.

Again, we'll save this as *watercooler.py*. Right now it doesn't do much of anything, but the methods are in place. SprintHandler will be used to define the websocket interactions through the open, on_message, and on_close methods, which are currently just stubbed out with docstrings.

 Starting with 4.0, Tornado denies cross-origin websocket connections by default through the check_origin. The preceding server will run on Tornado prior to 4.0, but this check will not be enforced.

The server runs on port 8080. Executing the script will start the server.

```
hostname $ python watercooler.py
```

Like Django's development server, this server can be stopped with Ctrl + C. Nothing catches the KeyboardInterrupt, so the console will output a stacktrace as follows:

```
hostname $ python watercooler.py
^CTraceback (most recent call last):
File "watercooler.py", line 31, in <module>
    IOLoop.instance().start()
...
KeyboardInterrupt
```

Don't worry; this is normal and will be handled soon. Unlike Django's development server, this server doesn't have any helpful output by default. It also doesn't autoreload when the code changes. We can enable these types of features in *watercooler.py* by using the debug flag in the application settings.

```
from urllib.parse import urlparse

from tornado.ioloop import IOLoop
from tornado.options import define, parse_command_line, options        ❶
from tornado.web import Application
from tornado.websocket import WebSocketHandler


define('debug', default=False, type=bool, help='Run in debug mode')    ❷
define('port', default=8080, type=int, help='Server port')
define('allowed_hosts', default="localhost:8080", multiple=True,
        help='Allowed hosts for cross domain connections')


class SprintHandler(WebSocketHandler):
    """Handles real-time updates to the board."""
```

```
    def check_origin(self, origin):                                    ❸
        allowed = super().check_origin(origin)
        parsed = urlparse(origin.lower())
        matched = any(parsed.netloc == host for host in options.allowed_hosts)
        return options.debug or allowed or matched

    def open(self, sprint):
        """Subscribe to sprint updates on a new connection."""

    def on_message(self, message):
        """Broadcast updates to other interested clients."""

    def on_close(self):
        """Remove subscription."""


if __name__ == "__main__":
    parse_command_line()                                               ❹
    application = Application([
        (r'/(?P<sprint>[0-9]+)', SprintHandler),
    ], debug=options.debug)                                            ❺
    application.listen(options.port)
    IOLoop.instance().start()
```

❶ These are new imports for the Tornado utilities for handling command-line arguments.

❷ Here we define the options that are available on the command line. Options can be mapped to a Python type. In this case, debug is either True or False and the port should be an integer. allowed_hosts can be passed multiple times.

❹ parse_command_line needs to be called for the options to be populated. Options that are not given on the command line will be populated with the defaults given by define.

❺ debug is passed to the application instance, and the port number is used to start the application.

❸ check_origin has been updated to use the new allowed_hosts and debug setting.

Enabling debug will provide logging output for requests coming to the server, including the status code they received and the response time. The code will also reload when *watercooler.py* is saved. As with Django, syntax errors on save and reload will cause the server to crash, and it will have to be manually restarted.

The allowed_hosts option domains can be used for cross-domain connections. This will allow connections from the local server or any server configured using the --allowed_hosts option on the command line. When debug is enabled, it will allow connections from any server.

 As with Django, it is not recommended to run the Tornado server with debug enabled in a production environment.

To handle stopping the server, the server will listen for the SIGINT signal sent during the keyboard interrupt. Here are the updates needed to *watercooler.py*:

```
import logging                                                      ❶
import signal
import time

from urllib.parse import urlparse

from tornado.httpserver import HTTPServer                            ❷
...

def shutdown(server):                                               ❸
    ioloop = IOLoop.instance()
    logging.info('Stopping server.')                                ❹
    server.stop()

    def finalize():
        ioloop.stop()
        logging.info('Stopped.')                                    ❺

    ioloop.add_timeout(time.time() + 1.5, finalize)


if __name__ == "__main__":
    parse_command_line()
    application = Application([
        (r'/(?P<sprint>[0-9]+)', SprintHandler),
    ], debug=options.debug)
    server = HTTPServer(application)                                ❻
    server.listen(options.port)
    signal.signal(signal.SIGINT, lambda sig, frame: shutdown(server))   ❼
    logging.info('Starting server on localhost:{}'.format(options.port))  ❽
    IOLoop.instance().start()
```

❶ ❷ These are new imports from the standard library and the Tornado HTTP server module.

❸ This function shuts down the HTTP server. It starts by stopping the server from accepting new connections; then, after a brief timeout, it stops the IOLoop completely.

❻ Rather than using `application.start`, an HTTP server instance is constructed with the application and started.

❼ The server that was created is bound to a signal handler for the SIGINT. When the signal is caught, it will call the previous shutdown code.

❹ ❺ This code sets up logging to provide insight into the current server state.
❽

> This example is based on common examples of graceful shutdown in the Tornado community, but it is not without flaws. It waits 1.5 seconds before stopping completely, which may not be sufficient for the existing requests to be completed. More detail on stopping a Tornado server can be found at *https://groups.google.com/forum/#!topic/python-tornado/VpHp3kXHP7s* and *https://gist.github.com/mywaiting/4643396*.

With these improvements in place, the server can be run in debug mode with more output and a more graceful exit.

```
hostname $ python watercooler.py --debug
[I 140620 21:56:23 watercooler:49] Starting server on localhost:8080
```

Again we can use Ctrl + C to stop:

```
hostname $ python watercooler.py --debug
[I 140620 21:56:23 watercooler:49] Starting server on localhost:8080
^C[I 140620 21:56:24 watercooler:31] Stopping server.
[I 140620 21:56:26 watercooler:36] Stopped.
```

We could make more improvements here, including binding on additional addresses, enabling HTTPS, or handling additional OS signals such as SIGTERM or SIGQUIT. This additional features would likely be needed to move this into a production environment. Those improvements should be straightforward based on the existing example and are left as an exercise for you. For now we are ready to add functionality to this server and make it handle client connections in a meaningful way.

Going forward, we'll assume that the server is running on the default port 8080 with the debug flag enabled.

Message Subscriptions

When a new client connects to *http://localhost:8080/1/*, the `SprintHandler.open` will be called, passing the value 1 as the sprint. As with Django, the URLs are routed using regular expressions and the named groups are translated into the arguments. New messages can be sent to the client at any point via the `write_message` method. The server needs to subscribe to the client to get any updates relevant to the sprint and when tasks in this sprint are updated. For a first implementation, the subscriptions can be tracked in the server `Application`. We'll create a subclass of `Application` that holds the list of subscribers for each sprint in a dictionary.

```python
import logging
import signal
import time

from collections import defaultdict                              ❶
from urllib.parse import urlparse
...
class ScrumApplication(Application):

    def __init__(self, **kwargs):
        routes = [
            (r'/(?P<sprint>[0-9]+)', SprintHandler),
        ]
        super().__init__(routes, **kwargs)
        self.subscriptions = defaultdict(list)                   ❷

    def add_subscriber(self, channel, subscriber):               ❸
        self.subscriptions[channel].append(subscriber)

    def remove_subscriber(self, channel, subscriber):            ❹
        self.subscriptions[channel].remove(subscriber)

    def get_subscribers(self, channel):                          ❺
        return self.subscriptions[channel]


def shutdown(server):
    ioloop = IOLoop.instance()
    logging.info('Stopping server.')
    server.stop()

    def finalize():
        ioloop.stop()
        logging.info('Stopped.')

    ioloop.add_timeout(time.time() + 1.5, finalize)


if __name__ == "__main__":
    parse_command_line()
    application = ScrumApplication(debug=options.debug)          ❻
    server = HTTPServer(application)
    server.listen(options.port)
    signal.signal(signal.SIGINT, lambda sig, frame: shutdown(server))
```

```
        logging.info('Starting server on localhost:{}'.format(options.port))
        IOLoop.instance().start()
```

❶ ❷ A new dictionary will be created to store the subscriptions when the application
❻   instance is created. The dictionary will map the sprint ID to a list of connections.
The routes are also constructed here rather than being passed in when the
application is created.

❸ ❹ Rather than exposing the underlying subscriptions dictionary, the application
❺   exposes the add_subscriber, remove_subscriber, and get_subscribers
methods for manipulating and querying the available subscribers. This
abstraction will make it easier to refactor later.

Holding the subscriptions like this works because the server application is a single process and single thread. Each handler has access to the application instance through its
application attribute. When a new client connects, the handler should register the
client to get updates about the relevant sprint, as shown here in *watercooler.py*.

```
...
class SprintHandler(WebSocketHandler):
    """Handles real-time updates to the board."""
...
    def open(self, sprint):
        """Subscribe to sprint updates on a new connection."""
        self.sprint = sprint
        self.application.add_subscriber(self.sprint, self)
...
```

If a client closes the connection, then the client should be removed from the list of
subscribers. In *watercooler.py*, this looks like:

```
...
class SprintHandler(WebSocketHandler):
    """Handles real-time updates to the board."""
...
    def on_close(self):
        """Remove subscription."""
        self.application.remove_subscriber(self.sprint, self)
...
```

This registers the client to get updates, but nothing yet handles those updates. When
the server gets a message from one of its clients, it needs to broadcast that message to
all of the interested clients. Since the application is tracking all of the subscriptions, it
can handle this broadcast as well, as shown here in *watercooler.py*.

```
...
from tornado.websocket import WebSocketHandler, WebSocketClosedError
...
class ScrumApplication(Application):
...
    def broadcast(self, message, channel=None, sender=None):
```

```
            if channel is None:
                for c in self.subscriptions.keys():
                    self.broadcast(message, channel=c, sender=sender)
            else:
                peers = self.get_subscribers(channel)
                for peer in peers:
                    if peer != sender:
                        try:
                            peer.write_message(message)
                        except WebSocketClosedError:
                            # Remove dead peer
                            self.remove_subscriber(channel, peer)
    ...
```

This simply forwards the message exactly as it was sent from the client to all of its peers. The peers are any other clients that are interested in the same sprint. If there are none, then the message just disappears into the ether. Attempting to write to a connection that has already been closed raises a WebSocketClosedError. In the case that the exception is raised, then the peer is simply removed from the list of subscribers.

We can also broadcast a message to all client regardless of sprint by passing the channel=None. This feature won't be used by the websocket handler, but it will be used later when passing updates from the Django application.

When a handler receives a message, it will call the application to broadcast the message and pass itself as the sender to ensure that it isn't given the message right back, as shown here in *watercooler.py*.

```
    ...
    class SprintHandler(WebSocketHandler):
        """Handles real-time updates to the board."""
    ...
        def on_message(self, message):
            """Broadcast updates to other interested clients."""
            self.application.broadcast(message, channel=self.sprint, sender=self)
    ...
```

This works for now, but it has a number of limitations. To start, it doesn't scale beyond a single process. All of the subscriptions are managed in memory on this one application instance. There is also no obvious way to pass messages from the Django application to this server to communicate with the peers. These problems will be addressed later in the chapter.

Client Communication

So far we've looked only at the server side of the websocket connection, but it is a bidirectional connection. The browser clients need to connect, pass messages to the server, and handle messages sent by the server. First we'll look at how this API is defined

---

by the standard, and then we'll build a wrapper around it to better integrate with our existing Backbone application code.

Minimal Example

For the client, a websocket is a relatively simple API. We make new connections by creating a new `WebSocket`, and the socket actions are handled through these callback functions:

- onopen

- onmessage

- onclose

- onerror

```
var socket = new WebSocket('ws://localhost:8080/123');
socket.onopen = function () {
    console.log('Connection is open!');
    socket.send('ping');
};
socket.onmessage = function (message) {
    console.log('New message: ' + message.data);
    if (message.data == 'ping') {
        socket.send('pong');
    }
};
```

Since the server currently doesn't validate the sprint that is passed, this example just uses a hardcoded value of 123. To test the connection, ensure that the *watercooler.py* server is up and running:

```
hostname $ python watercooler.py
[I 140629 11:47:58 watercooler:86] Starting server on localhost:8080
```

and then open *http://localhost:8080*. You can test this by pasting the script into your preferred browser's developer tools console.

 http://localhost:8080 will give a 404 error because our application does not define this URL. However, you can still complete this example from this page.

Pasting in the first script should display the "Connection is open!" message in the console, as seen in Figure 7-1.

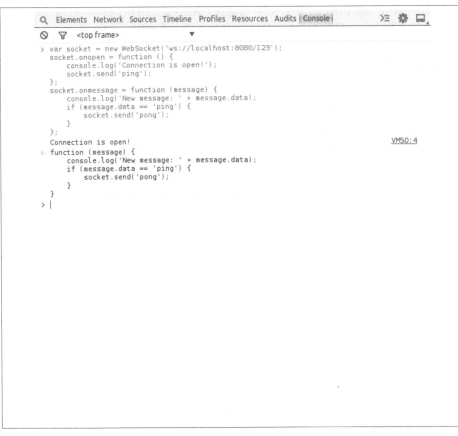

Figure 7-1. Initial websocket connection in browser developer tools

If you open another tab and paste this again, it will open up a new connection and you should see the two clients communicate. The newest tab will get a reply that says "pong," as seen in Figure 7-2.

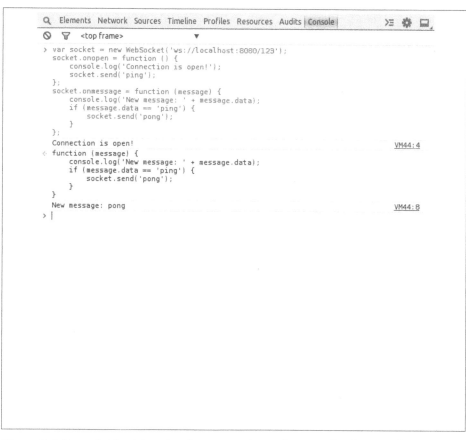

Figure 7-2. Second tab with websocket connection in browser developer tools

Going back to the original tab, you will see the "ping" message that was sent by the second tab, as shown in Figure 7-3.

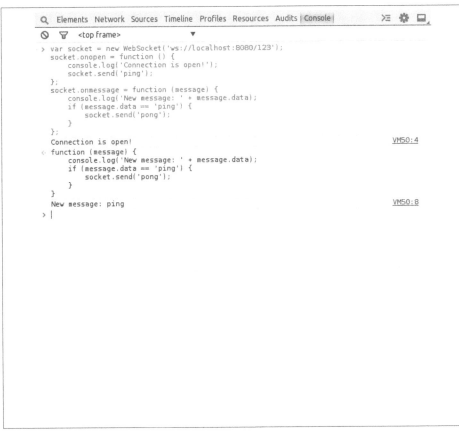

Figure 7-3. Original tab with websocket connection in browser developer tools

As this example demonstrates, the current server will blindly pass on any message to its related subscribers. For those messages to be meaningfully handled on the receiving end, they will need a more structured format. Next, we'll write a JS wrapper around this connection to translate the messages from the socket into Backbone events.

Socket Wrapper

The real-time communication will be used to notify the other clients about actions being taken on the frontend, such as a user currently dragging a task. To add structure to the messages, the clients will JSON-encode the messages. Each message will include the type of model being acted on, the ID of the model, and the action taken. These messages will be translated into Backbone events so that the views can subscribe to specific events rather than getting all messages from the websocket.

The encoding and translation of messages will be handled by a wrapper script to be created in *board/static/board/js/socket.js*.

```
(function ($, Backbone, _, app) {

    var Socket = function (server) {                                    ❶
        this.server = server;
        this.ws = null;
        this.connected = new $.Deferred();
        this.open();
    };

    Socket.prototype = _.extend(Socket.prototype, Backbone.Events, {
        open: function () {                                             ❷
            if (this.ws === null) {
                this.ws = new WebSocket(this.server);
                this.ws.onopen = $.proxy(this.onopen, this);
                this.ws.onmessage = $.proxy(this.onmessage, this);
                this.ws.onclose = $.proxy(this.onclose, this);
                this.ws.onerror = $.proxy(this.onerror, this);
            }
            return this.connected;
        },
        close: function () {
            if (this.ws && this.ws.close) {
                this.ws.close();
            }
            this.ws = null;
            this.connected = new $.Deferred();
            this.trigger('closed');
        },
        onopen: function () {                                           ❸
            this.connected.resolve(true);
            this.trigger('open');
        },
        onmessage: function (message) {                                 ❹
            var result = JSON.parse(message.data);
            this.trigger('message', result, message);
            if (result.model && result.action) {                       ❺
                this.trigger(result.model + ':' + result.action,
                    result.id, result, message);
            }
        },
        onclose: function () {                                          ❻
            this.close();
        },
        onerror: function (error) {                                     ❼
            this.trigger('error', error);
            this.close();
        },
        send: function (message) {                                      ❽
            var self = this,
```

```
                payload = JSON.stringify(message);
            this.connected.done(function () {
                self.ws.send(payload);
            });
        }
    });

    app.Socket = Socket;

})(jQuery, Backbone, _, app);
```

❶ The constructor takes the socket location to open, sets up the initial state to track, and opens the socket.

❷ open constructs the actual websocket instance if it hasn't already been created and binds all of the socket events to local methods of the same name.

❸ ❹ onopen, onmessage, onclose, and onerror handle the websocket events and
❻ ❼ translate them to similarly named events. They also maintain the connection state of the socket itself.

❺ onmessage handles decoding the messages from the server. It sends a blanket message event when a message is received but also sends namespaced messages for each model action.

❽ send handles encoding the messages sent to the server. It uses the connected state to ensure that messages aren't sent to a closed socket or before it is open.

This will translate messages of the form:

```
{
    model: 'modelname',
    id: 'id',
    action: 'actionname'
}
```

to events namespaced *modelname:actionname* and pass the id value as the first argument of the event handler. Subscribers can then listen for a specific subset of messages and all other messages.

To make this utility available on the client side, we need to add it to the *index.html* template (under *board/templates/board*).

```
...
<script id="config" type="text/json">
    {
        "models": {},
        "collections": {},
        "session": null,
        "views": {},
        "router": null,
        "apiRoot": "{% url 'api-root' %}",
```

```
        "apiLogin": "{% url 'api-token' %}"
    }
</script>
<script src="{% static 'board/js/app.js' %}"></script>
<script src="{% static 'board/js/socket.js' %}"></script>                ❶
...
```

 This is a reference to the previous socket wrapper script. It needs to come after the *app.js* configuration but before *views.js*, which needs to use it.

The next step is to integrate this wrapper into the current views.

Client Connection

The client needs to know the location of the websocket to make the connection. The server location could be passed in the configuration data like the apiRoot and apiLogin urls. That is a simple static approach to the configuration. A more dynamic approach would be to include this location as part of the API response. It could be its own resource, or for this application, a subresource of the sprints. To pass this information to the client, the SprintSerializer will be modified to pass this as another link. The Django application will need to know the location of the websocket server, which we can add with a new setting in *scrum/settings.py*.

```
...
STATIC_URL = '/static/'

WATERCOOLER_SERVER = os.environ.get('WATERCOOLER_SERVER', 'localhost:8080')

WATERCOOLER_SECURE = bool(os.environ.get('WATERCOOLER_SECURE', ''))
```

This defaults to *http://localhost:8080*, but can be configured via the WATERCOOLER_SERVER environment variable in a potential production deployment. By default, this will not expect the server to use a secure protocol, but it can also be configured.

The SprintSerializer can build the websocket URL from this setting and the sprint being requested, as shown here in *board/serializers.py*.

```
...
from django.conf import settings
from django.contrib.auth import get_user_model
...

class SprintSerializer(serializers.ModelSerializer):
...
    def get_links(self, obj):
        request = self.context['request']
        return {
            'self': reverse('sprint-detail',
                kwargs={'pk': obj.pk}, request=request),
```

```
            'tasks': reverse('task-list',
                request=request) + '?sprint={}'.format(obj.pk),
            'channel': '{proto}://{server}/{channel}'.format(
                proto='wss' if settings.WATERCOOLER_SECURE else 'ws',
                server=settings.WATERCOOLER_SERVER,
                channel=obj.pk
            ),
    }
```

The advantage to this approach is that while the server location is currently static, it could be made dynamic to load-balance the websocket connections. This approach also allows for changing the path construction without modifying the client, as well as making it easier to secure the websocket endpoint. Again, this isn't the only possible approach. This application centers the usage of the websocket on sprints, but if that usage were expanded it might make sense for the websocket channels to be their own resource in the API.

The client is going to track when users are dragging tasks on the sprint detail page. Remember that this page is controlled by the SprintView defined in *board/static/board/js/views.js*. To begin, the socket connection should be created when the view is initialized and closed when the view is removed.

```
...
var SprintView = TemplateView.extend({
    templateName: '#sprint-template',
    initialize: function (options) {
        var self = this;
        TemplateView.prototype.initialize.apply(this, arguments);
        this.sprintId = options.sprintId;
        this.sprint = null;
        this.tasks = {};
        this.statuses = {
            unassigned: new StatusView({
                sprint: null, status: 1, title: 'Backlog'}),
            todo: new StatusView({
                sprint: this.sprintId, status: 1, title: 'Not Started'}),
            active: new StatusView({
                sprint: this.sprintId, status: 2, title: 'In Development'}),
            testing: new StatusView({
                sprint: this.sprintId, status: 3, title: 'In Testing'}),
            done: new StatusView({
                sprint: this.sprintId, status: 4, title: 'Completed'})
        };
        this.socket = null;                                         ❶
        app.collections.ready.done(function () {
            app.tasks.on('add', self.addTask, self);
            app.sprints.getOrFetch(self.sprintId).done(function (sprint) {
                self.sprint = sprint;
                self.connectSocket();                               ❷
                self.render();
                // Add any current tasks
```

```
                app.tasks.each(self.addTask, self);
                // Fetch tasks for the current sprint
                sprint.fetchTasks();
            }).fail(function (sprint) {
                self.sprint = sprint;
                self.sprint.invalid = true;
                self.render();
            });
            // Fetch unassigned tasks
            app.tasks.getBacklog();
        });
    },
    ...
    connectSocket: function () {                                    ❸
        var links = this.sprint && this.sprint.get('links');
        if (links && links.channel) {
            this.socket = new app.Socket(links.channel);
        }
    },
    remove: function () {                                           ❹
        TemplateView.prototype.remove.apply(this, arguments);
        if (this.socket && this.socket.close) {
            this.socket.close();
        }
    }
});
...
```

 Initialize the socket attribute of the view when it is created.

❷ ❸ Once the sprint has been fetched, call a new method to connect. connectSocket will pull the location of the websocket from the API response.

❹ Override the default remove method to close the socket if one was open.

With the websocket connection now available, the client can now begin to broadcast events detailing the user's actions. These actions will be broadcast over the socket using the format described previously.

Sending Events from the Client

Currently, the application allows for adding new tasks to the backlog, but nothing allows the user to change the status column of a task. The user should be able to drag and drop tasks from one column to another. While the user is dragging the task, the application will broadcast the start and end of the drag so that other clients viewing the sprint will be able to update the status.

HTML5 introduced a JavaScript API for element drag-and-drop. It has good support for most desktop browsers, while mobile browsers are lagging. The API centers on new events fired by elements at different points in the process. Data can also be attached to the dragging element to give more context when handling the final drop.

 http://www.html5rocks.com/en/tutorials/dnd/basics/ is a good resource for the basics of the API. *http://caniuse.com/#feat=dragndrop* includes more information about browser support for native drag-and-drop.

Recall that each task is rendered by a `TaskItemView` defined in *views.js*. These are the elements that the user can drag and drop and will need to handle the events. However, `TaskItemView` doesn't have access to the socket. Either the `SprintView` needs to pass the socket down to these subviews, or the subviews need to trigger events that can be caught by the parent view that can access the socket. Using events allows for a better separation of responsibilities and will be the approach we use here in *board/static/board/js/views.js*.

```
...
var TaskItemView = TemplateView.extend({
    tagName: 'div',
    className: 'task-item',
    templateName: '#task-item-template',
    events: {
        'click': 'details',
        'dragstart': 'start',                                    ❶
        'dragenter': 'enter',
        'dragover': 'over',
        'dragleave': 'leave',
        'dragend': 'end',
        'drop': 'drop'
    },
    attributes: {                                                ❷
        draggable: true
    },
    ...
    start: function (event) {                                    ❸
        var dataTransfer = event.originalEvent.dataTransfer;
        dataTransfer.effectAllowed = 'move';
        dataTransfer.setData('application/model', this.task.get('id'));
        this.trigger('dragstart', this.task);
    },
    enter: function (event) {                                    ❹
        event.originalEvent.dataTransfer.effectAllowed = 'move';
        event.preventDefault();
        this.$el.addClass('over');
    },
    over: function (event) {                                     ❺
        event.originalEvent.dataTransfer.dropEffect = 'move';
        event.preventDefault();
```

```
            return false;
        },
        end: function (event) {                                    ❻
            this.trigger('dragend', this.task);
        },
        leave: function (event) {                                  ❼
            this.$el.removeClass('over');
        },
        drop: function (event) {                                   ❽
            var dataTransfer = event.originalEvent.dataTransfer,
                task = dataTransfer.getData('application/model');
            if (event.stopPropagation) {
                event.stopPropagation();
            }
            task = app.tasks.get(task);
            if (task !== this.task) {
                // TODO: Handle reordering tasks.
            }
            this.trigger('drop', task);
            this.leave();
            return false;
        }
    });
    ...
```

❶ These are the new events defined by the drag-and-drop API and will be bound to similarly named methods on the view.

❷ The draggable=true attribute is also part of the API and denotes that the element is draggable.

❸ The start event is fired when the user picks the element to start moving it. The client will store the current task ID to be used later when the element is dropped.

❹❺ The enter/over events are fired when another element is being dragged over the current element. Preventing the event tells the browser that the element can be dropped. This also adds a new class to visually indicate the element currently over this element.

❼ The leave event corresponds to the element moving out of the drop area for the current element. The class added when the element was moved over is now removed.

❻ The end event is triggered when the element being dragged stops but is not dropped in a new location.

❽ Finally, the drop event is fired when the element is dropped to a new location. This event will be fired by the drop target, not the original element being moved. Here the data context is used to check that the element was not dropped on itself.

The new over class can be handled with a small amount of CSS in *board/static/board/css/board.css*:

```
...

[draggable=true] {
    cursor: move;
}

.tasks .task-item.over {
    opacity: 0.5;
    border: 1px black dotted;
}
```

The task elements now allow for dragging and dropping onto one another. The logic of updating the model state is not yet implemented and will be handled later, but for now there are new events to be handled by the SprintView. Each task will fire dragstart, dragend, and drop events during the process. The SprintView needs to listen to these events and broadcast them to other clients that are viewing the same sprint. We'll need to reconfigure the renderTask method in *board/static/board/js/views.js* in order to utilize this new interaction.

```
...
var SprintView = TemplateView.extend({
    templateName: '#sprint-template',
...
    renderTask: function (task) {
        var view = new TaskItemView({task: task});
        _.each(this.statuses, function (container, name) {
            if (container.sprint == task.get('sprint') &&
                container.status == task.get('status')) {
                container.addTask(view);
            }
        });
        view.render();
        view.on('dragstart', function (model) {               ❶
            this.socket.send({
                model: 'task',
                id: model.get('id'),
                action: 'dragstart'
            });
        }, this);
        view.on('dragend', function (model) {                 ❷
            this.socket.send({
                model: 'task',
                id: model.get('id'),
                action: 'dragend'
            });
        }, this);
        view.on('drop', function (model) {                    ❸
            this.socket.send({
```

```
                model: 'task',
                id: model.get('id'),
                action: 'drop'
            });
        }, this);
        return view;
    },
    ...
```

❶ ❷ When the view triggers the drag events, they are passed on to the socket. Recall
❸   that the task is passed to the event handler as the first argument.

By using events in the subview, we can contain the logic of handling the socket connection and the format of messages in a single location. There is another drag-and-drop
case we need to handle, however. Currently, the tasks can be moved only onto other
tasks. This doesn't allow for moving the task into a new status column. The `StatusView`
needs to handle some of the drag-and-drop events to allow for this case in *board/static/
board/js/views.js*.

```
    ...
    var StatusView = TemplateView.extend({
        tagName: 'section',
        className: 'status',
        templateName: '#status-template',
        events: {
            'click button.add': 'renderAddForm',
            'dragenter': 'enter',                                        ❶
            'dragover': 'over',
            'dragleave': 'leave',
            'drop': 'drop'
        },
        ...
        enter: function (event) {                                        ❷
            event.originalEvent.dataTransfer.effectAllowed = 'move';
            event.preventDefault();
            this.$el.addClass('over');
        },
        over: function (event) {                                         ❸
            event.originalEvent.dataTransfer.dropEffect = 'move';
            event.preventDefault();
            return false;
        },
        leave: function (event) {                                        ❹
            this.$el.removeClass('over');
        },
        drop: function (event) {                                         ❺
            var dataTransfer = event.originalEvent.dataTransfer,
                task = dataTransfer.getData('application/model');
            if (event.stopPropagation) {
                event.stopPropagation();
            }
```

```
    // TODO: Handle changing the task status.
    this.trigger('drop', task);
    this.leave();
  }
});
...
```

❶ Since the user can't drag the column itself, the dragstart and dragend events don't need to be handled. Also, unlike the TaskItemView, this view is not marked as draggable.

❷ ❸ As with the TaskItemView, a new class is added or removed when the task
❹ element is over the column. Preventing the dragover event tells the browser that this is a valid drop location.

❺ Finally, the status column needs to handle the task drop using the data attached to the event. The logic for updating the task will be handled later.

The visual indication of the task being over the column is added by the over class on the status column in *board/static/board/css/board.css*:

```
...
.tasks .status.over {
    border: 1px black dotted;
}
```

Since the status columns are only drop targets and cannot be moved themselves, there is only one new event trigger. This indicates that the task has been dropped into the column. The SprintView in *board/static/board/js/views.js* needs to be updated to listen for this event.

```
...
var SprintView = TemplateView.extend({
    templateName: '#sprint-template',
    initialize: function (options) {
        var self = this;
        TemplateView.prototype.initialize.apply(this, arguments);
        this.sprintId = options.sprintId;
        this.sprint = null;
        this.tasks = {};
        this.statuses = {
            unassigned: new StatusView({
                sprint: null, status: 1, title: 'Backlog'}),
            todo: new StatusView({
                sprint: this.sprintId, status: 1, title: 'Not Started'}),
            active: new StatusView({
                sprint: this.sprintId, status: 2, title: 'In Development'}),
            testing: new StatusView({
                sprint: this.sprintId, status: 3, title: 'In Testing'}),
            done: new StatusView({
                sprint: this.sprintId, status: 4, title: 'Completed'})
```

```
    };
    _.each(this.statuses, function (view, name) {
        view.on('drop', function (model) {                          ❶
            this.socket.send({
                model: 'task',
                id: model.get('id'),
                action: 'drop'
            });
        }, this);
    }, this);
    ...
```

❶ The view listens to each StatusView instance for its drop event and broadcasts
a message about which task was dropped.

This event is broadcast with the same format as the previous events. Before we update
this code to write the task updates to the API, let's look at how another connected client
would handle these events on the other end.

Handling Events from the Client

The SprintView has now established the websocket connection when it loads and
broadcasts events when the user begins and completes a drag-and-drop action. If there
is another user viewing the same sprint, the socket will get the message on the websocket,
but nothing in the SprintView is listening for these messages.

What should the SprintView do when it receives a message from the websocket? As
shown here in *board/static/board/js/views.js*, it should give the original user some visual
indication that another user is modifying the task and potentially prevent other users
from trying to modify it at the same time.

```
    ...
    var TaskItemView = TemplateView.extend({
    ...
        lock: function () {                                          ❶
            this.$el.addClass('locked');
        },
        unlock: function () {
            this.$el.removeClass('locked');
        }
    });
    ...
    var SprintView = TemplateView.extend({
    ...
        connectSocket: function () {
            var links = this.sprint && this.sprint.get('links');
            if (links && links.channel) {
                this.socket = new app.Socket(links.channel);
                this.socket.on('task:dragstart', function (task) {  ❷
                    var view = this.tasks[task];
```

```
                    if (view) {
                        view.lock();
                    }
                }, this);
                this.socket.on('task:dragend task:drop', function (task) {        ❸
                    var view = this.tasks[task];
                    if (view) {
                        view.unlock();
                    }
                }, this);
            }
        },
    ...
```

❶   lock and unlock are new methods on the TaskItemView that add or remove a
    class to indicate that the task is being modified by another user. If there were an
    additional state to prevent modification while the task is locked, it could be
    toggled here.

❷   The socket listens for a drag to start on a task, looks up the relevant subview,
    and locks it.

❸   When the drag has ended either with or without a drop, the subview is unlocked.

The *board.css* file (in *board/static/board/css*) needs a small update for this new class.

```
...
.tasks .task-item.locked {
    opacity: 0.5;
}
```

This will give users a visual indication that the task is being moved by another user. The
client doesn't currently enforce any other restrictions to prevent another user from
modifying the same task, but it could do so in the lock/unlock methods. The application
could also handle editing a task in the same fashion. TaskItemView would fire an event
to indicate that the user has started the edit, the SprintView would pass this event to
the websocket, and when other clients receive the message, the task could be locked or
otherwise indicated to the user. When the edit was complete, another event would be
fired.

To see this working, you need two browser windows open and viewing the same sprint
page. When you start to drag a task in one window, the other window should change
the opacity of the task you are dragging. When it is dropped, the task should return to
normal.

The task:drop messages let the client know that another user has moved a task, but
they don't provide enough context for the client to determine where the task was moved.
In fact, currently the task status hasn't been updated when this event fires. We will
address that now.

Updating Task State

When we created the drop handlers in `TaskItemView` and `StatusView`, there were `TODO` items to handle the update of the task state. What state needs to be updated exactly? The column when the task is dropped determines the new task status. Changing the status might also change some of the dates tracked on the model, such as when it was started or completed. Tasks are ordered in each column, and moving the tasks should also allow for reordering them. To capture some of this logic, we will add a new helper to the `Task` model in *board/static/board/js/models.js*.

```
...
app.models.Task = BaseModel.extend({
...
    moveTo: function (status, sprint, order) {                        ❶
        var updates = {
            status: status,
            sprint: sprint,
            order: order
        },
        today = new Date().toISOString().replace(/T.*/g, '');
        // Backlog Tasks                                              ❷
        if (!updates.sprint) {
            // Tasks moved back to the backlog
            updates.status = 1;
        }
        // Started Tasks                                             ❸
        if ((updates.status === 2) ||
            (updates.status > 2 && !this.get('started'))) {
            updates.started = today;
        } else if (updates.status < 2 && this.get('started')) {
            updates.started = null;
        }
        // Completed Tasks                                           ❹
        if (updates.status === 4) {
            updates.completed = today;
        } else if (updates.status < 4 && this.get('completed')) {
            updates.completed = null;
        }
        this.save(updates);
    }
});
```

❶ This method takes three pieces of information: the new status, the new sprint, and the new order. Additional updates to the task state will be computed from these values.

❷ Tasks being assigned to the backlog will have their status reset to 1, which means "Not Started."

❸   If the task is being marked as started and the start date isn't set on the task, then it will be set to the current date. Likewise, if the task hasn't been started and the date is set, it will be cleared.

❹   Similar to the newly started tasks, the completion date will be set when a task is marked as complete. It will be cleared if the task is later moved out of the completed status.

The `TaskItemView.drop` handles the case of a task being dropped onto another task. When a task is dropped onto another task, it should be ordered to be in front of the current task. If the tasks are in different status columns, then the task will need to update its status as well. Tasks moved out of the backlog should be assigned to the current sprint. This snippet from *board/static/board/js/views.js* demonstrates.

```
...
var TaskItemView = TemplateView.extend({
    drop: function (event) {
        var self = this,
            dataTransfer = event.originalEvent.dataTransfer,
            task = dataTransfer.getData('application/model'),
            tasks, order;
        if (event.stopPropagation) {
            event.stopPropagation();
        }
        task = app.tasks.get(task);
        if (task !== this.task) {
            // Task is being moved in front of this.task
            order = this.task.get('order');
            tasks = app.tasks.filter(function (model) {                    ❶
                return model.get('id') !== task.get('id') &&
                    model.get('status') === self.task.get('status') &&
                    model.get('sprint') === self.task.get('sprint') &&
                    model.get('order') >= order;
            });
            _.each(tasks, function (model, i) {                            ❷
                model.save({order: order + (i + 1)});
            });
            task.moveTo(                                                   ❸
                this.task.get('status'),
                this.task.get('sprint'),
                order);
        }
        this.trigger('drop', task);
        this.leave();
        return false;
    },
    ...
```

❶   This gets all tasks that match the current sprint status and have an order greater than the current task.

❷　Each matched task will have its order increased by one.

❸　The dropped task will be moved to match the sprint and status and order of the task onto which it was moved.

Recall that this event is fired by the drop target, and `this.task` is the task being dropped onto, and `task` is the task being moved by the user. This handles a task being moved onto another task. The `StatusView.drop`, shown here in *board/static/board/js/ views.js*, handles the case when the task is dropped onto the column, which may or may not be empty.

```
...
var StatusView = TemplateView.extend({
    drop: function (event) {
        var dataTransfer = event.originalEvent.dataTransfer,
            task = dataTransfer.getData('application/model'),
            tasks, order;
        if (event.stopPropagation) {
            event.stopPropagation();
        }
        task = app.tasks.get(task);
        tasks = app.tasks.where({sprint: this.sprint, status: this.status});   ❶
        if (tasks.length) {
            order = _.min(_.map(tasks, function (model) {
                return model.get('order');
            }));
        } else {
            order = 1;
        }
        task.moveTo(this.status, this.sprint, order - 1);                       ❷
        this.trigger('drop', task);
        this.leave();
    }
});
...
```

❶　This finds all tasks matching the current column sprint and status and iterates over these tasks to get the smallest order.

❷　The task is updated to the sprint and status for the status view. Its order is set to one less than the smallest order found so all of the tasks don't need to be reordered. This allows only for adding the task to the top of the list of tasks in the column.

This updates the model state, but does not actually move the task HTML from one status column to another. To handle that, we'll need to update the `SprintView` (*in board/static/ board/js/views.js*) to handle changes to the task model.

```
...
var SprintView = TemplateView.extend({
```

```
        templateName: '#sprint-template',
        initialize: function (options) {
            ...
            app.collections.ready.done(function () {
                app.tasks.on('add', self.addTask, self);
                app.tasks.on('change', self.changeTask, self);                    ❶
                app.sprints.getOrFetch(self.sprintId).done(function (sprint) {
                    ...
                });
            },
            ...
            changeTask: function (task) {                                          ❷
                var changed = task.changedAttributes(),
                    view = this.tasks[task.get('id')];
                if (view && typeof(changed.status) !== 'undefined' ||
                    typeof(changed.sprint) !== 'undefined') {
                    view.remove();
                    this.addTask(task);
                }
            }
        }
    });
    ...
```

❶ When the SprintView is initialized, it binds to the change handler for the app.tasks collection. This is a collection of all tasks currently stored on the client.

❷ When any task changes, the changeTask callback fires. If the task is new to the current SprintView instance and either the status or sprint changed, the current view for the task is removed and the add handler is fired again to place it in the correct status column, if any.

With these changes in place, the task will be moved in the DOM when dropped, but this will not be reflected by other clients. When these drop events fire, they could pass the new status, sprint, and order values. However, in the case of dropping a task onto another task, potentially all of the tasks in the column need to be reordered and they would all need to be updated. The client could refetch all of the tasks, but there would be a race condition between when the API updates are completed and when the fetch is initiated. It would be better if the Django application could broadcast updates when the saves were complete. In the next chapter, we'll look at how the Django application can push updates to the client through the Tornado server.

CHAPTER 8

Communication Between Django and Tornado

In the previous chapter we created a Tornado-based server for handling websocket connections that can pass messages from client to client. In this chapter we'll expand on that server to allow the Django application to push updates, improve the security of the websocket connection, and incorporate Redis as a message broker to improve the future scalability of the server.

Receiving Updates in Tornado

To prevent the race condition described in the previous chapter that occurs when tasks are dropped versus updated in the API, the Django server needs a way to push updates to the Tornado server. The Django server currently knows the location of the server via the WATERCOOLER_SERVER setting, but as previously noted the Tornado server manages all of its client subscriptions and broadcasts internally, so there is no way to broadcast a message from outside Tornado.

In later sections we will update the server to use Redis as a message broker for this broadcast. In that case, Django could publish the message directly to Redis. However, that would require the Django application to know the format of messages and how the messages are broadcast by Tornado, which would break our well-defined interactions between the two servers.

How do we solve this problem? In order to keep these applications independent, the Tornado server will expose its own HTTP API to receive updates from Django. When the Tornado server receives an update, it will translate the update into the necessary format and broadcast it to any interested clients.

This endpoint will be handled by a new UpdateHandler in *watercooler.py*.

```
import json                                                          ❶
import logging
import signal
import time
...
from tornado.web import Application, RequestHandler                  ❷
...
class UpdateHandler(RequestHandler):
    """Handle updates from the Django application."""

    def post(self, model, pk):                                      ❸
        self._broadcast(model, pk, 'add')

    def put(self, model, pk):                                       ❹
        self._broadcast(model, pk, 'update')

    def delete(self, model, pk):                                    ❺
        self._broadcast(model, pk, 'remove')

    def _broadcast(self, model, pk, action):
        message = json.dumps({
            'model': model,
            'id': pk,
            'action': action,
        })
        self.application.broadcast(message)                         ❻
        self.write("Ok")


class ScrumApplication(Application):

    def __init__(self, **kwargs):
        routes = [
            (r'/(?P<sprint>[0-9]+)', SprintHandler),
            (r'/(?P<model>task|sprint|user)/(?P<pk>[0-9]+)', UpdateHandler),  ❼
        ]
        super().__init__(routes, **kwargs)
        self.subscriptions = defaultdict(list)
...
```

❶ ❷ These are new imports for json from the standard library and the Tornado
RequestHandler.

❸ ❹ UpdateHandler accepts POST, PUT, and DELETE requests mapping to add,
❺ update, and remove actions, respectively.

❻ Since the channel is not specified in the broadcast call, it will be sent to all
connected clients.

❼ UpdateHandler is added to the application routes. The model and pk arguments
are validated by the URL pattern regular expression.

The Tornado server now exposes an endpoint under */task/* to allow Django to push updates about new tasks or updated tasks. The endpoint has been kept generic enough to be used for the other application models.

Sending Updates from Django

The Django application needs to be updated to send the appropriate requests to notify the websocket server each time one of the models is created, updated, or deleted. This can be accomplished with the `post_save` and `pre_delete` hooks provided by `django-rest-framework`. Since this update will be added to all of the API views, it will be implemented as a mixin class in *board/views.py*.

```python
import requests                                              ❶

from django.conf import settings
from django.contrib.auth import get_user_model
...
class UpdateHookMixin(object):
    """Mixin class to send update information to the websocket server."""

    def _build_hook_url(self, obj):
        if isinstance(obj, User):
            model = 'user'
        else:
            model = obj.__class__.__name__.lower()
        return '{}://{}/{}/{}'.format(
            'https' if settings.WATERCOOLER_SECURE else 'http',
            settings.WATERCOOLER_SERVER, model, obj.pk)

    def _send_hook_request(self, obj, method):
        url = self._build_hook_url(obj)
        try:
            response = requests.request(method, url, timeout=0.5)
            response.raise_for_status()
        except requests.exceptions.ConnectionError:
            # Host could not be resolved or the connection was refused
            pass
        except requests.exceptions.Timeout:
            # Request timed out
            pass
        except requests.exceptions.RequestException:
            # Server responsed with 4XX or 5XX status code
            pass

    def post_save(self, obj, created=False):
        method = 'POST' if created else 'PUT'
        self._send_hook_request(obj, method)

    def pre_delete(self, obj):
        self._send_hook_request(obj, 'DELETE')
```

```
class SprintViewSet(DefaultsMixin, viewsets.ModelViewSet):
    ...
```

❶   Like the example Python client used in earlier chapters, this will use the `requests`
     library to construct the request to the Tornado server.

This mixin handles the `post_save` and `pre_delete` hooks for the API handler and
translates those into requests to the websocket server. It needs the `pre_delete` rather
than `post_delete` so that the object pk will still be available. There is a short timeout
to prevent the hook from blocking the API response for too long. Similarly, most of the
exceptions are suppressed. Here they've been blocked out in case additional logging or
handling would be needed for each case.

With the mixin complete, it needs to be added to the class definition of `SprintView`
`Set`, `TaskViewSet`, and `UserViewSet` in *board/views.py*.

```
...
class SprintViewSet(DefaultsMixin, UpdateHookMixin, viewsets.ModelViewSet):     ❶
    """API endpoint for listing and creating sprints."""

    queryset = Sprint.objects.order_by('end')
    serializer_class = SprintSerializer
    filter_class = SprintFilter
    search_fields = ('name', )
    ordering_fields = ('end', 'name', )


class TaskViewSet(DefaultsMixin, UpdateHookMixin, viewsets.ModelViewSet):       ❷
    """API endpoint for listing and creating tasks."""

    queryset = Task.objects.all()
    serializer_class = TaskSerializer
    filter_class = TaskFilter
    search_fields = ('name', 'description', )
    ordering_fields = ('name', 'order', 'started', 'due', 'completed', )


class UserViewSet(DefaultsMixin, UpdateHookMixin, viewsets.ReadOnlyModelViewSet):  ❸
    """API endpoint for listing users."""

    lookup_field = User.USERNAME_FIELD
    lookup_url_kwarg = User.USERNAME_FIELD
    queryset = User.objects.order_by(User.USERNAME_FIELD)
    serializer_class = UserSerializer
    search_fields = (User.USERNAME_FIELD, )
```

❶ ❷ Each `ViewSet` is given another base class of `UpdateHookMixin` to trigger the
❸   updates to the websocket server.

An alternate approach would be to use Django's signal handlers, which follow a similar API. With that method every model save and delete operation could be handled, not just those generated by API requests. There are advantages and disadvantages to this approach. One advantage is that clients can receive updates created outside the API, such as background jobs. The major disadvantage is that this approach adds overhead to each model save by potentially broadcasting changes when no client is listening. By broadcasting only changes created by the API, this overhead is added only when at least one client is using the API.

Handling Updates on the Client

At this point the Django application will notify the Tornado server when there are model changes, and Tornado will broadcast those changes to all connected clients. However, nothing on the client is currently listening for the <model>:add, <model>:update, or <model>:remove events. We can add this functionality to the SprintView in *board/static/board/js/views.js*.

```
...
var SprintView = TemplateView.extend({
...
    connectSocket: function () {
        var links = this.sprint && this.sprint.get('links');
        if (links && links.channel) {
            this.socket = new app.Socket(links.channel);
            this.socket.on('task:dragstart', function (task) {
                var view = this.tasks[task];
                if (view) {
                    view.lock();
                }
            }, this);
            this.socket.on('task:dragend task:drop', function (task) {
                var view = this.tasks[task];
                if (view) {
                    view.unlock();
                }
            }, this);
            this.socket.on('task:add', function (task, result) {          ❶
                var model = app.tasks.push({id: task});
                model.fetch();
            }, this);
            this.socket.on('task:update', function (task, result) {       ❷
                var model = app.tasks.get(task);
                if (model) {
                    model.fetch();
                }
            }, this);
            this.socket.on('task:remove', function (task) {               ❸
                app.tasks.remove({id: task});
            }, this);
```

```
        }
    },
    ...
```

❶ Tasks are fetched when the add event is seen.

❷ Tasks are updated if they are found in the collection. Since the updates are broadcast to all clients, a task might be updated outside of the current sprint that doesn't need to be updated.

❸ When tasks are deleted, they are removed from the collection.

These changes register the SprintView to handle task updates. Nothing in the application allows for modifying users, and while new sprints can be added, that isn't relevant to the user when viewing the details for this sprint. If those events were needed, the subscriptions could be added in a similar fashion.

Now when a task is dropped to a new status or reordered in a status column, all connected clients should get the update and move the task. To test this again, you will need two browser windows open and viewing the same sprint. When the drop is complete in the first browser, both browsers should move the task to the new status column.

When the client receives an event about a new task or an edit, the client refetches the task from the API. This is inefficient for the client that made the original addition or edit, since it will refetch the task information it already has. It also means that all clients will make the same API call around the same time, creating a mini–denial-of-service attack on our own server. These problems will be addressed in later sections.

Server Improvements

The real-time updates for the tasks are now fully functional when we are viewing the details of a sprint, but as noted in previous sections there are a few places on our Tornado server where there is still room for improvement. Lightweight does not mean insecure, nor does it mean nonrobust.

Robust Subscriptions

One problem with the Tornado server implementation is that it doesn't scale beyond a single process. All of the subscription information and message broadcast handling is done in memory by the application instance. While a single Tornado process is built to handle numerous concurrent connections with a single process, having a single process is not very fault tolerant. In the current configuration, if there is more than one instance it won't be aware of all clients that might need messages.

To resolve this issue, the server will use Redis as a message broker. Redis (*http://redis.io/*) is a popular key-value store that also has support for pub-sub (publish-subscribe) channels. While Redis isn't a true message broker like RabbitMQ or ActiveMQ, it is easy to install and administer and can be used as a message queue for the simple messaging patterns needed here. There is also great support for integrating Redis with Tornado. You can refer to the Redis documentation for information on how to install and configure it for your local system.

Interacting with Redis will require the `tornado-redis` library from PyPi. `tornado-redis` recommends using the synchronous Redis client to publish messages to a channel, so `redis-py` should also be installed.

```
hostname $ pip install tornado-redis redis
```

`tornado-redis` has built-in classes for managing a pub-sub channel when you are using SockJS or Socket.IO. Since this project is using websockets without those abstractions, we need a simple extension of the provided `BaseSubscriber`. We will add this to *watercooler.py*. `ScrumApplication` and its related subscription methods will also need to be updated to use this `RedisSubscriber`.

 `hiredis` is a Redis client written in C, and the Python bindings are available on PyPi. `redis-py` will use the `hiredis` parser if it is installed and can provide a speed improvement. It does need to compile on install, so you will need a compiler and the Python headers for your platform prior to attempting installation.

```
...
from redis import Redis
from tornado.httpserver import HTTPServer
from tornado.ioloop import IOLoop
from tornado.options import define, parse_command_line, options
from tornado.web import Application, RequestHandler
from tornado.websocket import WebSocketHandler
from tornadoredis import Client
from tornadoredis.pubsub import BaseSubscriber


class RedisSubscriber(BaseSubscriber):                                    ❶

    def on_message(self, msg):
        """Handle new message on the Redis channel."""
        if msg and msg.kind == 'message':
            subscribers = list(self.subscribers[msg.channel].keys())
            for subscriber in subscribers:
                try:
                    subscriber.write_message(msg.body)
                except tornado.websocket.WebSocketClosedError:
                    # Remove dead peer
                    self.unsubscribe(msg.channel, subscriber)
        super().on_message(msg)
```

```
...
class ScrumApplication(Application):

    def __init__(self, **kwargs):
        routes = [
            (r'/(?P<sprint>[0-9]+)', SprintHandler),
            (r'/(?P<model>task|sprint|user)/(?P<pk>[0-9]+)', UpdateHandler),
        ]
        super().__init__(routes, **kwargs)
        self.subscriber = RedisSubscriber(Client())                          ❷
        self.publisher = Redis()                                             ❸

    def add_subscriber(self, channel, subscriber):
        self.subscriber.subscribe(['all', channel], subscriber)              ❹

    def remove_subscriber(self, channel, subscriber):
        self.subscriber.unsubscribe(channel, subscriber)                     ❺
        self.subscriber.unsubscribe('all', subscriber)

    def broadcast(self, message, channel=None, sender=None):                 ❻
        channel = 'all' if channel is None else channel
        self.publisher.publish(channel, message)
...
```

❶ The new Redis client to handle pub-sub channel subscriptions and pass the relevant messages on to the subscribed websocket handlers. This is assuming that the Redis server is running on a local server using the default port with no authentication. The list of subscribers is copied in case subscribers need to be removed during iteration.

❷❸ The previous in-memory subscriptions dictionary has been replaced by two Redis connections: an asynchronous client for managing the subscriptions and a synchronous one for broadcasting new messages.

❹ The signature of add_subscriber remains the same, but it now subscribes the connection to two Redis channels: one for the current sprint name and one for messages being sent to all clients.

❺ Similarly, remove_subscriber changes very little, but it must unsubscribe the connection to the new all channel.

❻ broadcast has been changed to use the all channel when the channel isn't specified. sender is unused, but we will fix this later.

Since the method signatures on ScrumApplication have remained the same, none of the calls in SprintHandler need to change.

The use of the new all channel is required because the ScrumApplication no longer knows the names of all of the channels in the case of multiple websocket servers. There is a small problem introduced here, which is that because the RedisSubscriber doesn't know which `SprintHandler` (if any) put the message on the channel, a client will receive its own message back. The JS client could put an identifier in the message body so that it can choose to ignore messages that originated from itself. Or each `SprintHandler` could do the same. This project will handle this at the server (in *watercooler.py*) to reduce the amount of traffic on the websocket.

```python
import json
import logging
import signal
import time
import uuid                                                    ❶
...
class RedisSubscriber(BaseSubscriber):

    def on_message(self, msg):
        """Handle new message on the Redis channel."""
        if msg and msg.kind == 'message':
            try:                                               ❷
                message = json.loads(msg.body)
                sender = message['sender']
                message = message['message']
            except (ValueError, KeyError):
                message = msg.body
                sender = None
            subscribers = list(self.subscribers[msg.channel].keys())
            for subscriber in subscribers:
                if sender is None or sender != subscriber.uid:
                    try:
                        subscriber.write_message(message)
                    except tornado.websocket.WebSocketClosedError:
                        # Remove dead peer
                        self.unsubscribe(msg.channel, subscriber)
        super().on_message(msg)
...
class SprintHandler(WebSocketHandler):
    """Handles real-time updates to the board."""

    def open(self, sprint):
        """Subscribe to sprint updates on a new connection."""
        # TODO: Validate sprint
        self.sprint = sprint.decode('utf-8')
        self.uid = uuid.uuid4().hex                            ❸
        self.application.add_subscriber(self.sprint, self)
...
class ScrumApplication(Application):
...
    def broadcast(self, message, channel=None, sender=None):
        channel = 'all' if channel is None else channel
        message = json.dumps({                                 ❹
            'sender': sender and sender.uid,
            'message': message
```

```
    })
    self.publisher.publish(channel, message)
...
```

❶ This is a new standard library import uuid.

❸ Each connection handler generates a unique ID when the connection is opened.

❹ When a message is broadcast, it is wrapped to annotate its original sender if there was one.

❷ When a message is received on the channel, it is unwrapped to get the original message and the sender. If there was no sender, the message is sent to all subscribers. Otherwise, it is sent to all subscribers other than the original sender.

Now the Tornado server can be scaled beyond a single process by making use of Redis as a simple message broker. While the scalability of the server has improved, however, there are still places where the server could be made more secure.

Websocket Authentication

There is currently no validation for the sprint ID, which is passed to the SprintHandler instance. This is bad for a couple of reasons. First, it opens the server to be used for any message forwarding. When the server is deployed to a production server and exposed on the public Internet, any two clients can connect to a random integer sprint and pass messages over the socket. Second, a malicious client can connect to the channel for an actual sprint ID and broadcast incorrect messages, causing connected clients to think there are updates when there are not. Adding this validation will serve to authenticate the clients to prevent misuse.

To resolve this, the websocket server and the Django server will share a secret that can be used to pass information between the two. Recall that the API response for a sprint tells the client the location of the websocket. This allows the API to include a token in the websocket URL. When the client opens the websocket, it can verify the token using the shared secret.

Here we add a new setting to track this shared secret between the API and websocket servers in *scrum/settings.py*.

```
...
WATERCOOLER_SERVER = os.environ.get('WATERCOOLER_SERVER', 'localhost:8080')

WATERCOOLER_SECURE = bool(os.environ.get('WATERCOOLER_SECURE', ''))

WATERCOOLER_SECRET = os.environ.get('WATERCOOLER_SECRET',
    'pTyz1dzMeVUGrb0Su4QXsP984qTlvQRHpFnnlHuH')
```

As with the SECRET_KEY setting, this should be a randomly generated string. The preceding string is used only for example purposes.

This secret can be used by the SprintSerializer to generate a token for the websocket and is included in the response, as shown here in *board/serializers.py*.

```
...
from django.conf import settings
from django.contrib.auth import get_user_model
from django.core.signing import TimestampSigner                        ❶
...
class SprintSerializer(serializers.ModelSerializer):
...
    def get_links(self, obj):
        request = self.context['request']
        signer = TimestampSigner(settings.WATERCOOLER_SECRET)          ❷
        channel = signer.sign(obj.pk)
        return {
            'self': reverse('sprint-detail',
                kwargs={'pk': obj.pk}, request=request),
            'tasks': reverse('task-list',
                request=request) + '?sprint={}'.format(obj.pk),
            'channel': '{proto}://{server}/socket?channel={channel}'.format(
                proto='wss' if settings.WATERCOOLER_SECURE else 'ws',
                server=settings.WATERCOOLER_SERVER,
                channel=channel,
            ),
        } ❸
```

❶ ❷ The channel is generated using Django's cryptographic signing utilities and the shared websocket secret.

❸ The channel communicates the channel for the sprint, which still uses the primary pk as the identifier.

The TimestampSigner is used to sign the channel name, which prevents it from being tampered with on the client side. Since it is timestamped, this token can be short-lived and prevents reuse if captured. The format of the URL has been changed and the Tornado server will need to be updated to reflect this change. However, because the client uses this URL directly from the API, this update does not require any changes to the JS client.

More information on Django's signing utilities can be found here: *https://docs.djangoproject.com/en/1.7/topics/signing/*.

The Tornado server needs to be updated in *watercooler.py* to handle this change. It needs to capture the channel from the query parameter and verify the signature. The application needs to be configured with its shared secret as well.

```python
import json
import logging
import os
...

from django.core.signing import TimestampSigner, BadSignature, SignatureExpired   ❶
from redis import Redis
...

class SprintHandler(WebSocketHandler):
    """Handles real-time updates to the board."""

    def check_origin(self, origin):
        allowed = super().check_origin(origin)
        parsed = urlparse(origin.lower())
        matched = any(parsed.netloc == host for host in options.allowed_hosts)
        return options.debug or allowed or matched

    def open(self):                                                               ❷
        """Subscribe to sprint updates on a new connection."""
        self.sprint = None
        channel = self.get_argument('channel', None)
        if not channel:
            self.close()
        else:
            try:
                self.sprint = self.application.signer.unsign(                     ❸
                    channel, max_age=60 * 30)
            except (BadSignature, SignatureExpired):
                self.close()
            else:
                self.uid = uuid.uuid4().hex
                self.application.add_subscriber(self.sprint, self)

    def on_message(self, message):
        """Broadcast updates to other interested clients."""
        if self.sprint is not None:                                              ❹
            self.application.broadcast(message, channel=self.sprint, sender=self)

    def on_close(self):
        """Remove subscription."""
```

```
        if self.sprint is not None:                                    ❺
            self.application.remove_subscriber(self.sprint, self)
    ...
    class ScrumApplication(Application):

        def __init__(self, **kwargs):
            routes = [
                (r'/socket', SprintHandler),                           ❻
                (r'/(?P<model>task|sprint|user)/(?P<pk>[0-9]+)', UpdateHandler),
            ]
            super().__init__(routes, **kwargs)
            self.subscriber = RedisSubscriber(Client())
            self.publisher = Redis()
            self._key = os.environ.get('WATERCOOLER_SECRET',           ❼
                'pTyz1dzMeVUGrb0Su4QXsP984qTlvQRHpFnnlHuH')
            self.signer = TimestampSigner(self._key)
    ...
```

❶ ❼ A new TimestampSigner is created and attached to the global application when it is created. It pulls the shared secret from the OS environment. This must match the secret used by the Django application.

❷ Instead of being pulled from the URL path, the channel name is pulled from the channel parameter. If the channel isn't given, then the connection is immediately closed.

❸ The value for the channel is pulled from the signed value. If the signature fails or has expired, the connection is closed.

❻ The URL is updated to a more generic /socket/ since the channel name is now passed through the query string.

❹ ❺ on_message and on_close need to handle the case where the sprint is None.

By the time the open method is called, the connection has already been accepted and the client's onopen callback has fired. This creates a small window for a newly opened client to try to send messages before the channel signature can be verified. We handle this by setting self.sprint to None and checking that it has been properly set prior to broadcasting messages or adding and removing subscriptions.

Currently the token will expire in 30 minutes. Ideally this could be shorter, but because the token is generated when the sprint is fetched on the home page, there might be a long delay between when it is used on the sprint detail page. We could improve this by making another API call to generate the channel URL right before it is needed. In that case, the timeout could be made shorter.

Here Django is used as a library rather than a framework to use only the signing utilities. This code sharing is one advantage of using a Python framework like Tornado to handle the websocket. It ensures that the implementations are kept in line.

This could be replaced by a generic signing library, such as `itsdang erous` (*https://pythonhosted.org/itsdangerous/*), as well.

The update endpoint also needs to be secured to ensure that only the Django application can push updates. We will address this next, along with other improvements to how the `UpdateHandler` processes the updates.

Better Updates

Currently when a user edits a task, either inline or by dragging and dropping it to a new status, that change is submitted to the API. The Django server then notifies the Tornado server, which tells all clients that there was an update. When the browser client sees that there is an update, it fetches the task information from the API. For the user who submitted the original request, this is a wasted API call. The other connected clients are all making the same API call to get the same information. It would be more efficient to send that information along to the clients through the websocket in the first place.

This requires updates in all three parts of the application. First, the Django application needs to be updated to send the current model state to the Tornado server. Recall that this is handled by the `UpdateHookMixin` in *board/views.py*.

```
...
from rest_framework import authentication, filters, permissions, viewsets
from rest_framework.renderers import JSONRenderer
...
class UpdateHookMixin(object):
    """Mixin class to send update information to the websocket server."""
...
    def _send_hook_request(self, obj, method):
        url = self._build_hook_url(obj)
        if method in ('POST', 'PUT'):                              ❶
            # Build the body
            serializer = self.get_serializer(obj)
            renderer = JSONRenderer()
            context = {'request': self.request}
            body = renderer.render(serializer.data, renderer_context=context)
        else:
            body = None
        headers = {
            'content-type': 'application/json',
        }
        try:
            response = requests.request(method, url,
                data=body, timeout=0.5, headers=headers)            ❷
            response.raise_for_status()
```

```
        except requests.exceptions.ConnectionError:
            # Host could not be resolved or the connection was refused
            pass
        except requests.exceptions.Timeout:
            # Request timed out
            pass
        except requests.exceptions.RequestException:
            # Server responded with 4XX or 5XX status code
            pass
    ...
```

❶ In the case of a new or updated task, the current model state is serialized in the
   same format used by the API and output as JSON.

❷ Here the previously constructed body is passed on to the Tornado update hook.

Previously, the Tornado server wasn't expecting any information in the request body.
UpdateHandler needs to be updated in *watercooler.py* to send this data along to the
client.

```
    ...
    class UpdateHandler(RequestHandler):
        """Handle updates from the Django application."""
    ...
        def _broadcast(self, model, pk, action):
            try:
                body = json.loads(self.request.body.decode('utf-8'))          ❶
            except ValueError:
                body = None
            message = json.dumps({
                'model': model,
                'id': pk,
                'action': action,
                'body': body,                                                 ❷
            })
            self.application.broadcast(message)
            self.write("Ok")
    ...
```

❶ The request body is decoded as JSON, if possible.

❷ Parsed body data is sent along to the clients through the websocket broadcast.

Finally the task:add and task:update handlers in the SprintView need to be updated
in *board/static/board/js/views.js* to use this body if it is given.

```
    ...
    var SprintView = TemplateView.extend({
    ...
        connectSocket: function () {
            ...
            this.socket.on('task:add', function (task, result) {
```

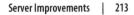

```
        var model
        if (result.body) {
            model = app.tasks.add([result.body]);                    ❶
        } else {
            model = app.tasks.push({id: task});
            model.fetch();
        }
    }, this);
    this.socket.on('task:update', function (task, result) {
        var model = app.tasks.get(task);
        if (model) {
            if (result.body) {
                model.set(result.body);                              ❷
            } else {
                model.fetch();
            }
        }
    }, this);
    ...
```

...

❶   The new task is added directly from the websocket data rather than bring fetched from the API.

❷   Similarly, the task data is updated from the websocket data rather than another update being made.

As previously noted, one critical issue with the Tornado webhook is that nothing secures this endpoint. Anyone with knowledge of the server location could push updates to all of the connected clients. This won't directly impact the database contents unless clients receive the bad model data and then later save it. The next section will address this security problem.

Secure Updates

There are a number of ways to add a security layer outside the application. An HTTP proxy, such as Nginx, could be placed in front of the server to enforce basic, digest, or client authentication. That authentication would need to be added to the request generated by the Django application. It's also possible to include some verification of the messages between the two servers using the existing shared secret. In the same way that the channel is signed for verification, the webhook requests can be signed to ensure that they came from a trusted endpoint and were not modified in transit.

This message verification is not a substitute for using encryption in the communication between the servers. In a production environment, the Tornado server should receive the updates over HTTPS.

The UpdateHookMixin will need to send a signature of the request it is sending, and the UpdateHandler will need to verify that signature before broadcasting the update. The verified value needs to include information about the model type and ID as well as the action (add, update, remove) and any additional data about the model state. Here is how this functionality looks in *board/views.py*:

```python
import hashlib                                                          ❶
import requests
...
from django.conf import settings
from django.core.signing import TimestampSigner                         ❷
from django.contrib.auth import get_user_model
...
class UpdateHookMixin(object):
...
    def _send_hook_request(self, obj, method):
        url = self._build_hook_url(obj)
        if method in ('post', 'put'):
            # Build the body
            serializer = self.get_serializer(obj)
            renderer = JSONRenderer()
            context = {'request': self.request}
            body = renderer.render(serializer.data, renderer_context=context)
        else:
            body = None
        headers = {
            'content-type': 'application/json',
            'X-Signature': self._build_hook_signature(method, url, body)   ❸
        }
        try:
            response = requests.request(method, url,
                data=body, timeout=0.5, headers=headers)
            response.raise_for_status()
        except requests.exceptions.ConnectionError:
            # Host could not be resolved or the connection was refused
            pass
        except requests.exceptions.Timeout:
            # Request timed out
            pass
        except requests.exceptions.RequestException:
            # Server responded with 4XX or 5XX status code
            pass

    def _build_hook_signature(self, method, url, body):                  ❹
        signer = TimestampSigner(settings.WATERCOOLER_SECRET)
        value = '{method}:{url}:{body}'.format(
            method=method.lower(),
            url=url,
            body=hashlib.sha256(body or b'').hexdigest()
        )
```

```
        return signer.sign(value)
    ...
```

❶ ❷ The `TimestampSigner` is used to generate a signature for the request based on
❹ the request method, URL, and the body.

❸ The signature is passed through the `X-Signature` header to the Tornado
endpoint.

The value of the signature depends on the current URL, the request method, and the
body. This prevents a valid signature from one request being used on another fake
request. Only the hash of the body is used to prevent the signature from being too large.
Again, it is timestamped to prevent the request from being replayed outside of the expiry
window, which will be kept very short.

 This signature derivation is a simplified version of how requests are
signed in the Amazon Web Services API. For more information on
the signing process, see *http://docs.aws.amazon.com/general/latest/gr/
signature-version-4.html*.

`UpdateHandler` needs to be updated in *watercooler.py* to verify this signature. Verifying
the signature requires checking both that the signature is signed correctly and that the
signed value contains the information matching the current request.

```
import hashlib                                                            ❶
import json
...
from django.core.signing import TimestampSigner, BadSignature, SignatureExpired
from django.utils.crypto import constant_time_compare                    ❷
...
from tornado.web import Application, RequestHandler, HTTPError            ❸
...
class UpdateHandler(RequestHandler):
...
    def _broadcast(self, model, pk, action):
        signature = self.request.headers.get('X-Signature', None)        ❹
        if not signature:
            raise HTTPError(400)
        try:
            result = self.application.signer.unsign(signature, max_age=60 * 1)  ❺
        except (BadSignature, SignatureExpired):
            raise HTTPError(400)
        else:
            expected = '{method}:{url}:{body}'.format(                   ❻
                method=self.request.method.lower(),
                url=self.request.full_url(),
                body=hashlib.sha256(self.request.body).hexdigest(),
            )
```

```
                if not constant_time_compare(result, expected):
                    raise HTTPError(400)
            try:
                body = json.loads(self.request.body.decode('utf-8'))
            except ValueError:
                body = None
            message = json.dumps({
                'model': model,
                'id': pk,
                'action': action,
                'body': body,
            })
            self.application.broadcast(message)
            self.write("Ok")
    ...
```

❶ ❷ These are new required imports for `hashlib`, `constant_time_compare`, and
❸   `HTTPError`.

❹   The signature is pulled from the headers, and a 400 response is returned if it
       wasn't found.

❺   The signature is verified as valid and not expired. The signature expires in one
       minute.

❻   The unsigned value is compared to its expected value.

The signature now ensures that the request to the update hook came from a server with
access to the shared secret. Again, the expiry is kept short to prevent the same request
from being replayed, but because it is so short the clocks on the two servers must be
kept in sync or this step will fail.

Final Websocket Server

Exactly how much work was it to create this websocket server? Let's look at the full
application code from *watercooler.py*:

```
import hashlib
import json
import logging
import os
import signal
import time
import uuid

from urllib.parse import urlparse

from django.core.signing import TimestampSigner, BadSignature, SignatureExpired
from django.utils.crypto import constant_time_compare
from redis import Redis
from tornado.httpserver import HTTPServer
```

```
from tornado.ioloop import IOLoop
from tornado.options import define, parse_command_line, options
from tornado.web import Application, RequestHandler, HTTPError
from tornado.websocket import WebSocketHandler
from tornadoredis import Client
from tornadoredis.pubsub import BaseSubscriber


define('debug', default=False, type=bool, help='Run in debug mode')
define('port', default=8080, type=int, help='Server port')
define('allowed_hosts', default="localhost:8080", multiple=True,
       help='Allowed hosts for cross domain connections')


class RedisSubscriber(BaseSubscriber):

    def on_message(self, msg):
        """Handle new message on the Redis channel."""
        if msg and msg.kind == 'message':
            try:
                message = json.loads(msg.body)
                sender = message['sender']
                message = message['message']
            except (ValueError, KeyError):
                message = msg.body
                sender = None
            subscribers = list(self.subscribers[msg.channel].keys())
            for subscriber in subscribers:
                if sender is None or sender != subscriber.uid:
                    try:
                        subscriber.write_message(message)
                    except tornado.websocket.WebSocketClosedError:
                        # Remove dead peer
                        self.unsubscribe(msg.channel, subscriber)
        super().on_message(msg)


class SprintHandler(WebSocketHandler):
    """Handles real-time updates to the board."""

    def check_origin(self, origin):
        allowed = super().check_origin(origin)
        parsed = urlparse(origin.lower())
        matched = any(parsed.netloc == host for host in options.allowed_hosts)
        return options.debug or allowed or matched

    def open(self):
        """Subscribe to sprint updates on a new connection."""
        self.sprint = None
        channel = self.get_argument('channel', None)
        if not channel:
            self.close()
```

```
        else:
            try:
                self.sprint = self.application.signer.unsign(
                    channel, max_age=60 * 30)
            except (BadSignature, SignatureExpired):
                self.close()
            else:
                self.uid = uuid.uuid4().hex
                self.application.add_subscriber(self.sprint, self)

    def on_message(self, message):
        """Broadcast updates to other interested clients."""
        if self.sprint is not None:
            self.application.broadcast(message, channel=self.sprint, sender=self)

    def on_close(self):
        """Remove subscription."""
        if self.sprint is not None:
            self.application.remove_subscriber(self.sprint, self)


class UpdateHandler(RequestHandler):
    """Handle updates from the Django application."""

    def post(self, model, pk):
        self._broadcast(model, pk, 'add')

    def put(self, model, pk):
        self._broadcast(model, pk, 'update')

    def delete(self, model, pk):
        self._broadcast(model, pk, 'remove')

    def _broadcast(self, model, pk, action):
        signature = self.request.headers.get('X-Signature', None)
        if not signature:
            raise HTTPError(400)
        try:
            result = self.application.signer.unsign(signature, max_age=60 * 1)
        except (BadSignature, SignatureExpired):
            raise HTTPError(400)
        else:
            expected = '{method}:{url}:{body}'.format(
                method=self.request.method.lower(),
                url=self.request.full_url(),
                body=hashlib.sha256(self.request.body).hexdigest(),
            )
            if not constant_time_compare(result, expected):
                raise HTTPError(400)
        try:
            body = json.loads(self.request.body.decode('utf-8'))
        except ValueError:
```

```python
            body = None
        message = json.dumps({
            'model': model,
            'id': pk,
            'action': action,
            'body': body,
        })
        self.application.broadcast(message)
        self.write("Ok")


class ScrumApplication(Application):

    def __init__(self, **kwargs):
        routes = [
            (r'/socket', SprintHandler),
            (r'/(?P<model>task|sprint|user)/(?P<pk>[0-9]+)', UpdateHandler),
        ]
        super().__init__(routes, **kwargs)
        self.subscriber = RedisSubscriber(Client())
        self.publisher = Redis()
        self._key = os.environ.get('WATERCOOLER_SECRET',
            'pTyz1dzMeVUGrb0Su4QXsP984qTlvQRHpFnnlHuH')
        self.signer = TimestampSigner(self._key)

    def add_subscriber(self, channel, subscriber):
        self.subscriber.subscribe(['all', channel], subscriber)

    def remove_subscriber(self, channel, subscriber):
        self.subscriber.unsubscribe(channel, subscriber)
        self.subscriber.unsubscribe('all', subscriber)

    def broadcast(self, message, channel=None, sender=None):
        channel = 'all' if channel is None else channel
        message = json.dumps({
            'sender': sender and sender.uid,
            'message': message
        })
        self.publisher.publish(channel, message)


def shutdown(server):
    ioloop = IOLoop.instance()
    logging.info('Stopping server.')
    server.stop()

    def finalize():
        ioloop.stop()
        logging.info('Stopped.')

    ioloop.add_timeout(time.time() + 1.5, finalize)
```

```
if __name__ == "__main__":
    parse_command_line()
    application = ScrumApplication(debug=options.debug)
    server = HTTPServer(application)
    server.listen(options.port)
    signal.signal(signal.SIGINT, lambda sig, frame: shutdown(server))
    logging.info('Starting server on localhost:{}'.format(options.port))
    IOLoop.instance().start()
```

Fewer than 200 lines create a server to handle both broadcasting events from client to client and also from server to clients. Our application was able to make use of existing Django utilities to verify the connected client and incoming requests. The two servers share a secret key.

This lightweight approach to real-time Django has a number of moving pieces, built over the previous few chapters. There is a RESTful API built in Django, a single-page application built with Backbone.js, and a websocket server using Tornado. Each piece has its own role, and there is well-defined communication between each service. The Django server interacts with the frontend application, with minimal configuration passed in the template and over the REST API. The Django application pushes updates to Tornado over a set HTTP endpoint. The clients interact with the websocket using a simple message pattern that is unknown to Django. Lightweight Django means thinking about Django as one piece of a larger puzzle and learning how to make it interact with other composable services.

Index

We'd like to hear your suggestions for improving our indexes. Send email to index@oreilly.com.

About the Authors

Julia Elman is a designer, developer, and tech education advocate based in North Carolina. She has been working on her brand of web skills since 2002. Her creative nature drove her to find work in 2007 at Hallmark Cards, Inc., where she worked on projects such as the Product (RED) campaign and Hallmark's site redesign. From there, she took a dive into Django as a junior designer/developer at World Online in Lawrence, Kansas. In early 2013, she helped start a local chapter of Girl Develop It and empowered over 850 members to learn computer programming. She also helped organize the 2013 Teen Tech Camp, where 20 local teens learned Python programming in a one-day event.

Mark Lavin has been a developer since 2006, first working on Wall Street and now as Technical Director of Caktus, the largest Django-specific development firm in the United States. He is an active member of the Django community, speaking at conferences, contributing to open source projects, and answering questions on StackOverflow. When not coding, he enjoys homebrewing, running, participating in Ironman triathlons, and spending time with his wife and their two young daughters at their home in Apex, North Carolina.

Colophon

The animals on the cover of *Lightweight Django* are vervain hummingbirds (*Mellisuga minima*). Native to Jamaica, Haiti, and the Dominican Republic, these non-migratory hummingbirds are common, favoring subtropical and tropical lowland forests.

While lacking the bright, jewellike plumage of other hummingbird species, they are notable for being the second smallest bird in the world, after the bee hummingbird of Cuba. The vervain measures roughly 2.4 inches in length, including its bill, and weighs between .07 and .08 ounces. These birds primarily feed on nectar from flowers, using their extendible tongues to lap up the nectar at a rate of 13 times per second.

Hummingbirds are solitary creatures, coming together only to breed. The male disperses immediately after copulation, leaving the female to build the nest and raise the young. These eggs are the smallest laid by any bird, at just a third of an inch in length, weighing .375 grams on average. Nests are barely the size of half a walnut shell.

Despite its diminutiveness, the vervain produces a loud, piercing song—often the only indication of its presence, as this bird can be difficult to spot due to its size. Highly vocal, the birds turn their heads from side to side as they sing.

Many of the animals on O'Reilly covers are endangered; all of them are important to the world. To learn more about how you can help, go to animals.oreilly.com.

The cover image is from *Wood's Natural History*. The cover fonts are URW Typewriter and Guardian Sans. The text font is Adobe Minion Pro; the heading font is Adobe Myriad Condensed; and the code font is Dalton Maag's Ubuntu Mono.

Have it your way.

Get even more for your money.

Join the O'Reilly Community, and register the O'Reilly books you own. It's free, and you'll get:

- $4.99 ebook upgrade offer
- 40% upgrade offer on O'Reilly print books
- Membership discounts on books and events
- Free lifetime updates to ebooks and videos
- Multiple ebook formats, DRM FREE
- Participation in the O'Reilly community
- Newsletters
- Account management
- 100% Satisfaction Guarantee

Signing up is easy:

1. Go to: oreilly.com/go/register
2. Create an O'Reilly login.
3. Provide your address.
4. Register your books.

Note: English-language books only

To order books online:
oreilly.com/store

For questions about products or an order:
orders@oreilly.com

To sign up to get topic-specific email announcements and/or news about upcoming books, conferences, special offers, and new technologies:
elists@oreilly.com

For technical questions about book content:
booktech@oreilly.com

To submit new book proposals to our editors:
proposals@oreilly.com

O'Reilly books are available in multiple DRM-free ebook formats. For more information:
oreilly.com/ebooks

CPSIA information can be obtained at www.ICGtesting.com
Printed in the USA
BVOW11s0321281114

376990BV00012B/50/P